Beautifully
Broken

Published in 2022 by Welford Publishing
Copyright © Cassandra Welford 2022

ISBN: Paperback 978-1-7390970-9-7

Author photograph © Rony Cadavid 2022
Editor Christine McPherson

A catalogue for this book is available from the British Library.

Beautifully Broken

A Welford Publishing Collaboration

She made broken look beautiful and strong look invincible.
She walked with the Universe on her shoulders and made it look like a pair of wings.

Ariana Dancu

Contents

Little Miss Misunderstood

Carolyn Parker

You may be familiar with the Mr Men and Little Miss series of books written by Roger Hargreaves. They were a favourite with my children, the most requested being Mr Tickle with his extraordinary long arms, long enough to reach out to tickle people on every page, which made my two girls giggle and wriggle and start to tickle each other. I don't think we ever got to the end of the book without them rolling around on the floor in fits of uncontrollable laughter!

I wonder what your favourite childhood book is.

I was brought up on the Winnie the Pooh series, with the wonderful mix of characters from wise Owl to woeful Eeyore and the honey-loving Pooh bear's adventures with his little friend Piglet. I loved nothing better, as a small child, than to sit on my mum's lap while she read to me.

I started life in a rather unconventional way, being adopted at the tender age of six weeks by a couple living in the small English town of Sutton Coldfield, before it was absorbed into Birmingham. My adoptive mum was 32, a housewife, trained in domestic science, and my adoptive father was a chartered accountant for Metals & Alloys, a local engineering business.

I was a much-wanted child, as they'd explored every available avenue to have their own baby, without success.

Their joy, however, was my birth mum's heartbreak. How she wished she could have kept me, how she held me night and day for those formative six weeks, knitting clothes for me to wear when I was collected on that excruciating day, only for them to be changed before I was taken away from the mother and baby unit in Warwickshire in a new-smelling carrycot, in a stranger's car with a new name, new identity, and no understanding as to where my mother's reassuringly familiar voice had gone. Did no-one realise that this sudden change of environment came with consequences, came with confusion and anxiety that would play out in the future?

I was Patricia, then I was Carolyn; I was comforted and breast fed by my mum with all her familiar noises and smells, then I was held in hands that could span an octave and two on the piano, and fed by a bottle with an unfamiliar tasting teat and milk. I slept in a place that was quiet, not full of other baby chatter, I was handed round and cooed over by strangers. I didn't know **who** I was, or **where** I was, or **what** had happened to the female voice that had held me close and spoken so kindly to me for six weeks, night and day.

No-one realised.

No-one thought of my inner emotional turmoil.

The social worker wrote in her report – and my adoptive mother often told me – that I was a good baby, that I didn't cry, yet they never understood or even wondered about the why, the shock, the coping mechanism of one so vulnerable and small, to be still, to be silent, to withdraw in an attempt to be safe.

Little Miss Misunderstood, as I think of my inner child now, lay on the rug of the suburban garden of number 27, surrounded by flowers, and guarded by another adoptee, Timmy – the Heinz-variety canine companion that had followed her new mother home from the bus one day and with whom she shared her new parents' affection.

My earliest memories are of wanting to have a sibling. How painful it must have been when I asked each Christmas for a baby brother or sister. How difficult it was for me to understand that this wasn't a possibility. After several years of no 'suitable' babies coming up for adoption, my parents had come off the waiting list as 'the age gap was becoming too big'. In reality, my mum had agreed to accept a mixed-race boy, but my father immediately threw this idea out. He was backed up, unusually, by my grandfather, and the subject wasn't ever mentioned again.

Little Miss Misunderstood (alias Little Miss Lonely) was brought up in an ordered way, her god-mother later remarking that it was akin to that of the

Von Trapp family regime, minus the whistle! Everyone remained oblivious to how this affected her.

The first time these effects appeared in a tangible way was at primary school; she had started school early, at the age of three-and-a-half. Having a great appetite for knowledge, she leapt ahead of her peers in this respect – to the pride of her parents but to her own chagrin. For although intellectually she was top of the class, in emotional maturity she lagged behind. Being the only only-child in the class also put her at a disadvantage when it came to making friends. Hers was a singularly isolated childhood, alone at home and lacking the skills to make friends at school, she felt left out, rejected, and different in some way.

One day, everyone was asked to bring a board game into school to play, as it was some kind of staff training day. She just wanted to play, to join in, but over and over again she was pushed out until the inner hurt and frustration became too much to hold in. She started tipping up game boards all around the class. The air was filled with flying coloured counters and cards. The transient sense of revenge was sweet. **Now** they were taking her seriously. **Now** she had the power to make them listen to her.

This victory, though, was short-lived.

She was soon dragged out of the classroom by the back of her collar and made to sit, crying, outside the headmistress's office. The punishment for such unruly behaviour was to be put into a younger class for the rest of the day and to be referred to as 'The

Naughty Girl'. Far from addressing her need to be heard and the inner turmoil to be acknowledged and understood, this approach only added another layer of trauma to her growing sense of being misunderstood.

When would anyone listen?

Many years went by.

Many times she tried to be part of the gang, but failed; to meet her parents' expectations, without success. The wins she achieved were marred by not being *quite* good enough. The nine O levels weren't grade A, the eight piano grades not a distinction, and nothing she did matched the level of the daughter of one of their bridge partners. How inadequate that made her feel; how jealous she was of that other girl.

This lonely, lost little girl, who desperately wanted to please her parents, became a young woman desperately seeking praise, looking for attention, searching for love and acceptance.

She was trapped again, but this time inside her soon-to-be adult self, still gagged, still trying to be heard. Her pride was wounded and her self-esteem in tatters. She yearned to be listened to, to be understood. Dreaming of achieving the dreams that seemed so far away, she cowered in the corner, her face in her hands wet with her tears. She vowed that someday, somehow, she would rise up and be ignored no more.

Trouble was brewing, a time bomb waiting to go off, but at this point no-one had an inkling of what was to come.

Have you watched a child trying to get its parents' attention, tugging at its mother's sleeve while saying, "Mum, Mum. Look, Mum!" when she's otherwise occupied, scrolling on her phone perhaps, oblivious of the minor intrusion of her child's tugging and voice in her mind?

What does the child do? It tugs harder and more insistently, while calling out louder and louder in an increasingly higher pitched voice.

Little Miss Misunderstood was no different. She was determined to make her feelings known, her voice heard, and to be noticed... one day.

Then one day...

She began to beat the ground with her fist and stamp her feet.

To scream and shout.

To throw things around.

To show her strength of feeling through fits of anger that burst out like an unexpected volcanic eruption.

Sudden. Explosive.

With words of hatred and frustration, in a torrent of pure rage.

Destroying anything within reach.

Bowls crashing to the ground.

Splinters of custard-spattered china skidding across the tiled kitchen floor.

An empty champagne bottle whirring through the air to bounce off the patio door.

…Before (and as abruptly as it began) she crumbled to her knees, hot tears springing from her eyes in frustration tinged with shame.

All the fight ebbed out from her limbs, limp and wrapped into a foetal pose – the pose most familiar to her.

Her adult mind disoriented and confused at the uncontrolled outburst, racing with questions, but mainly: *Why? And what to do?*

Pause. Breathe. Process.

Analyse. Wonder. Question.

What to do?

What to do, indeed?

This recurring behavioural pattern was a mystery. Years went by, one marriage and two children, before the roots finally began to be discovered.

Yet sadly, at the point of first seeking help, of being open and honest, judgment and talk of punishment pushed Little Miss Misunderstood deep underground, through fear and lack of trust.

When would anyone hear and wrap their arms around her? she wondered.

***

In September 2018, at the age of 59, I was introduced to the transformative power of personal development and having a growth mindset, through joining an amazing team of positive-minded people in a network marketing company. Once I began to be exposed to books and podcasts and others chatting about how to grow in confidence and self-belief, things really started to turn around.

By this stage in life, I had experienced one mental breakdown, three divorces, two abusive marriages, and had lost contact with my two children. I had been abused physically, emotionally, psychologically, sexually, and financially, and every shred of self-belief had been torn out of me. Even my loud-mouthed inner child had been silenced by such treatment; she had learnt that to raise her voice was to put my very existence in danger.

I was hungry for a way to change my life for the better, so I devoured all the information I could find and began to put it into practice. Rome wasn't built in a day, and the same is true of changing your inner conversations. There was a long list of negative beliefs about myself that needed to be faced and changed to more positive statements. Slowly, I began to speak kindly to myself and to flourish, to start to love myself again and see a future.

A future that was expansive and fun.

A future where I was loved and accepted.

A future where I could turn around my past and use it to help others.

As part of this healing journey, I signed up with a personal coach, who has been hugely instrumental in helping me to face and explore the past with its fears, emotions, and images, to forgive myself and others involved, and to release so much that was holding me captive. It was Tracey who introduced me to the concept of inner child work, for which I am eternally grateful.

I imagine Little Miss Misunderstood was also jumping with joy when she was finally recognised, her presence validated, and her need to be heard and understood met.

There are still times when I need reminding to check in with her – often when my reactions to a situation are childlike in nature. But when I take the time to journal and ask questions like *What is going on? What am I feeling? Where is this coming from? What is my inner child trying to tell me here?* I often get a flood of words and images that help me understand why I'm reacting like a petulant five-year-old.

Sometimes I just need to imagine I'm sitting with my inner child by my side or on my lap, listening to her and then reassuring her that everything is going to be alright, that there's no need to panic or be afraid.

For example, last summer I hit a metaphorical brick wall, due to an unexpected life event flooring me. All self-confidence just drained out of me, and I wanted to curl up in a ball and hide. I stopped interacting as much in my Facebook community, I stopped writing, I lost my sense of direction and motivation, and my vision of having a successful business clouded over. I eventually realised that I felt hurt, frustrated, and disappointed in myself. This was accompanied by the image of a child at the foot of this wall, banging her fists on the ground screaming, "It's not fair!!"

This was my inner child. You may recall me describing her in that pose earlier.

I started to write… Memories tumbled onto the pages of things that had happened through the years which had evoked the stinging feeling of 'not being fair'. I wrote until the words stopped, emotionally drained by the task.

I had listened. I understood. Afterwards, I wrote a letter of forgiveness in my journal, forgiving everyone involved in these events, and forgiving myself for my part in them.

I had let go and felt a deep sense of peace.

Finally, I asked my inner child what she needed, and again a list quickly filled my page. Simple things.

To be listened to.

To be heard.

To be understood.

For her thoughts, feelings, and opinions to be validated.

And most importantly, for me not to be ashamed of her.

I used to feel a bit weird when I spoke of my inner child, but now I speak openly about her. I guess she is chuffed at being the subject of this chapter! I also appreciate that at times she just needs a hug, as we all do when things are tough.

I would like to make a promise to my inner child that from now on:

She will be listened to.

She will be heard.

She will be understood.

Her thoughts, feelings, and opinions will be validated. And most importantly…

I will never be ashamed of her.

I hereby rename her, Little Miss Understood.

Inspirational Insight

Some of the positive steps I took to move forward...

Hearing and accepting that my inner child desperately wanted me to listen to her, calm and reassure her, and give her the self-love she lacked, without judgement, was the first huge step to wholeness, bringing us to a place of harmony with each other.

Like the child demanding its parents' attention, she had to take extreme measures for me to turn around and see her distress. Being aware of when she is hurt or fearful now, I know I need to sit and listen, to reassure and hold her in my mind's eye, as strange as this may sound.

The second biggest step I've taken is to shift the shame of the past outbursts by going public and sharing my story here. By talking to you and a worldwide audience about my inner child, I am demonstrating that I am no longer ashamed of her.

If you are going through any similar challenges, I want you to know...

firstly, you are NOT alone.

Many people, for fear of being wrongly branded as having some mental disorder – or of being totally misunderstood, as I was – keep quiet, never seeking out someone to help unlock the secrets, unpick the root cause of their behaviour, and facilitate them to discover and get to know their own inner child.

The suggestions that follow come from the inner work I did with my own coach over a period of two to three years. I use them in outline to this day when I catch myself wanting to react or think in a childlike way, rather than as an adult, to life's curveballs.

I found it useful to simply sit with the emotions and images that came up from my childhood, rather than push them away, only to surface again when triggered by the next challenge I faced.

As well as talking, as if to my five-year-old self, writing a letter to her was a powerful way to express my compassion and love towards her. It was emotional, for sure, and written with tears streaming down my face. Yet these were healing tears and words demonstrating that she was wanted, her feelings valid, important, and heard. This exercise went a long way towards healing the emotional wounds I experienced while growing up. The disconnect I experienced between child and adult gradually lessened, and now I feel we are in touch again.

If my story has touched *you*, or resonated in some way, then I would encourage you to give some thought to following this up. I know there are many books and online resources available, with an increasing number of coaches specialising in this area.

Maybe your inner child is tugging at your heart and wanting a listening ear.

I wish I had known...

that it's not wrong to look into these things. It's not occult or dangerous. Instead, it has been powerful and transformative, leading me to a greater understanding and love for myself, and a deep sense of inner peace.

I'm finally whole and not at war with myself.

Yet wholeness is a process, and I'm not done with learning to recognise when my inner child needs some tender loving care. But I'm definitely on the way.

I wish I had come across the principles of a growth mindset and personal development teachings earlier.

Now I know and truly believe:

I am OK.

I am always loveable.

I am enough.

I am accepted and respected.

It's OK to be me!

I was Beautifully Broken.

I am now a channel for others to gain insight from my life experiences, to know they're not alone, and to overcome adversity in their lives with the knowledge that there is always hope.

Dedication

To those whose inner child is longing to be recognised and heard.

To all who have supported me on my journey to wholeness; especially Tracey, my coach, who continues to walk alongside me as I unravel my past, encouraging me to spread my wings and fly.

About the Author

Carolyn, who lives in rural Leicestershire, England, has been described as compassionate, caring, and courageous, with a warm, welcoming smile.

When she's not supporting her senior sitting service clients, Carolyn can be found drinking in the sights and sounds of nature in the nearby countryside, or socialising with friends in her favourite cafe or pub. She has always been a 'people person', being known locally as the admin of a Facebook Covid19 community support group, set up in 2020.

Carolyn discovered the transformative power of mindset and personal development in 2019, and has steadily challenged and changed her beliefs, values, and behaviours, leading her to now be able to state: "I am a woman who knows, loves, and can be myself, without fear of judgment or shame. This is me."

Carolyn's mission is to leave a legacy by turning taboo topics that tainted her past into talking points, allowing for a conversation with and within the reader, as well as amongst those connected to others who have walked similar paths.

Connect with Carolyn

Carolyn is writing her debut heart-led book, *From A Place Called Shame*, which is due for publication in late 2022/early 2023.

Email: carolyn.parker@restoringselfbelief.co.uk

Facebook: **Restoring Self Belief**

Instagram: instagram.com/restoringselfbelief

Bereavement
& Blessings

Kate Fernandez

B ereavement and blessings may not be words that you'd usually associate together, but I would love to share my insight of life-changing and life-affirming events.

2002

My world fell apart in 2002, when my amazing, funny, and strong husband passed away after being diagnosed with a grade four brain tumour. In 2001, Stan underwent massive surgery, chemotherapy, and radiotherapy, which had a devastating effect on him. He rallied after the first surgery to stay with his family and friends. For me this was life-changing. I vividly recall sitting in his favourite chair, swaying backwards and forwards, overwhelmed and frightened for our two daughters, who were 17 and seven at the time. They were my reason to get up every morning and to keep going.

The year before my husband's death was harrowing in places, watching the person you love and have chosen to spend your life with disappear in front of your eyes is vile. Stan was known for his love of life and his energy, which would fill a room when he entered it.

The combination of drugs, surgery, and treatment changed his personality and his view of life. Stan was 50 when he died, and I was 34. We had only been married for eight years. This may seem a strange thing to say, but I learned so much for him in such a few short years of marriage. We had the opportunity to live in India and Dubai, and he travelled so much with his work. Stan was born in Delhi but moved to the UK with his family at the age of nine. I thought I would learn about India, Indian culture and traditions from a book, but that wasn't how it went. Stan was offered a job in India, and an incredible experience of a unique way of life unfolded. We later moved to Dubai, and Stan made sure that I knew how to be independent and be there for our daughters. He taught me the importance of family and looking out for one another. He taught me how to love, as various experiences in my life had tainted my view of love.

You might wonder where the blessing comes in this. Stan's surgery and treatments were incredibly aggressive, and he endured so much. But he taught me to be strong, and I needed that strength to carry on without him. I am so incredibly grateful for all his guidance and love.

After he died, I wanted and needed to do something gentle and kind. My daughters became my focus and reason to go on. They were the reason I got out of bed, even when I didn't want to. The simple things like cooking and washing and just holding it together seemed to be all I could manage. But I still needed to take the girls to school and college, and I am glad I did. I had amazing family and friends who checked in with us and helped where they could, but at times, I felt incredibly lost and lonely.

Family events were some of the hardest days. We celebrated Sarah's 18th birthday, and she went off to university in Swansea during that first year. Georgie had her first holy communion, and there was a big family wedding. All events where Stan wasn't there.

I remember at my nephew's wedding, as I sat down at the beginning of the service, it hit me that it was the first wedding I had attended without him. I sobbed and sobbed.

I think most of the time I just held onto my own grief and did my best to be there for my girls. When I look back, I realise there were many times I just didn't cope. I remember a dear friend arriving one day and taking Georgie for a few hours to do some baking, which she loved. I had been given strict and kind instructions to go back to bed and sleep! I think I just ran on autopilot.

After a few months, I decided to learn about aromatherapy and got a part-time job in a local shop. I felt this would be good for me and for my family. There were many personal challenges to deal with, but the aromatherapy course gave me something nurturing to focus on, and the part-time job meant I still had contact with people. Training as an aromatherapist was the first part of my healing journey.

Although it's been tough going at times, many beautiful memories have been made with my daughters over the last 20 years, including when I walked Sarah down the aisle on her wedding day. And I am thrilled that Georgie gets married this year. Seriously proud Mum moments!

Stan died on the 26th of May, 2002 – a date I will never forget. But now we celebrate on that day, too, as my beautiful granddaughter Sophie was born on 26th May, 2016! Sophie arrived much earlier than we had all expected, but her smiling face and beautiful energy and love of life fills my heart.

2012

2012 was the most challenging year of my own life, when I was diagnosed with a squamous cell carcinoma of my tongue. This was life-changing event no. 2!

In June 2012, I went through a total of 27 hours of surgery over three separate days. The first visit to theatre was scheduled, and the plan was to cut my tongue in half to remove the tumour which had grown on the left side of my tongue. Even the process of having investigations to confirm my cancer is something I vividly remember – searing pain from three biopsies, followed by an earth-shattering diagnosis a week later.

However, I think it would probably help if I explained what the amazing surgeons, anaesthetists, nurses, radiographers, and the team of ten specialists did to give me the best chance of getting over this diagnosis.

The surgery involved severing my tongue in half, rebuilding my tongue with the graft from my left arm with a nerve attached, and then repairing my arm with a graft from my stomach. I joke about having a tummy tuck at 44! The reason for the three visits to theatre was that the operation didn't work the first time, so they repeated the whole procedure. The second time round, it worked. And the last operation was to clear a blockage in my neck.

That final trip into theatre was my life-changing moment! I came back onto the ward with a nasal gastric tube, which was being used for drugs and liquid food. I felt like my whole identity had been lost and that I was just being fed and watered. I wanted some say in what was happening to me, so I yanked that tube out of my face with every ounce of energy I could muster. ENOUGH! This is my body, I reasoned, and I am deciding what happens to it.

After 17 difficult days in hospital, I was discharged, probably to the relief of the staff on the ward as well as myself. In the first few days after my surgery, I had a look at myself in a mirror, and I looked like I had been in a head-on collision, black, swollen, and disfigured. It was a sight that not only me, but my family and friends had to endure. I had a brief spell of time to recover myself, and started to learn to speak again, to eat, and to swallow. That all sounds simple, but it wasn't. My first meal back home was a curry (my choice), but the food had to be liquidised for me to attempt to eat it. So the path to eating and drinking again was one with lots of bumps along the way.

After a few weeks, part two of the process began, in the form of six weeks of radiotherapy appointments, with weekends off for good behaviour. This entailed a mask being made of my face, which was used to attach me to the radiotherapy bed so that the radiotherapy hit only the places it was meant to. It was horrendous at first, but I got used to it over the six-week period and concentrated on just marking off the days. I jest about weekends off, but most importantly this was time to rest. In some ways, the cumulative effect of the radiotherapy was harder to deal with than some of the surgery. You are burnt to a crisp and the pain is horrendous, but I got through it with the end goal of attending my cousin's wedding.

The team in the radiotherapy department thought I was crazy for planning to get to a wedding 21 days after my last treatment. But I did it, and wore two scarves and a big hat to hide my burns and scars.

The last ten years have been a healing journey of changing my diet and trying to reduce stress levels, although plenty has happened in that 10-year period to cause me stress, including the loss of my dad and close friends, as well as supporting my mum as her health deteriorated.

You probably wonder why I have written about my cancer under a heading of Bereavement and

Blessings, but I feel that my experience of having cancer held a sense of bereavement and loss – a loss of my health, of things I could no longer do, and of plans and dreams that didn't come to fruition. At times, I felt like I had completely lost my identity. There is also a sense of loss of the life you had before diagnosis.

However, the blessings that have come from my cancer journey are being cancer-free, committing to learning Reiki and other complementary therapies, understanding the benefits of these therapies, different foods, supplements, crystals, the healing power of nature, and the importance and immense value of self-care.

2022

So, life-changing event no. 3. It is just over a month since my beloved mum died out in Spain, a place she had called home for the last 22 years. Mum moved to Spain with her husband John, who I loved. He was sadly diagnosed with pancreatic cancer and died only a few short months after his diagnosis in 2008, and I helped Mum take care of him. My mum had battled with her own health, as her own mother did, but Mum was strong. She was diagnosed with breast cancer six weeks before my own cancer diagnosis, but Mum also had emphysema – a lung condition that causes shortness of breath and other health problems.

For many years, Mum required hours of oxygen daily. She didn't much like having to have an oxygen machine, whether that was at home or the portable one which became an integral part of her trips when she left the house. In fact, for the last six years of her life, she had treatment in Spain which helped, and I think the warmth of the sunshine there helped her, too.

I have so many different memories with my mum, but the happiest are of her on the amazing cruise around the Mediterranean which we did to celebrate her 80th birthday. It was a planning nightmare, but worth every second it took to organise with the amazing travel agent. Mum wore her beautiful clothes and shoes, and enjoyed a visit to the galley to see the kitchens which was perfect for a foodie like her. Mum was in awe of the sheer volume of staff, food, and equipment on board, and the food was amazing. I remember her wearing beautiful, vibrant Frank Usher dresses that she even wore when she was working in the kitchen of her award-winning restaurant. Mum also loved beautiful Gina Shoes and matching handbags; Imelda Marcos would have been proud!

Tennis was something my mum had a huge interest in, and when she had the restaurant the layout of the kitchen would always change in late June in time for Wimbledon. The new layout made space for a television in the corner so that Mum could keep up with the tennis! Mum also loved flowers, and the entrance to her apartment was a vision of colour throughout the year. As her health deteriorated and it became difficult for me to travel to Spain, partly down to the Covid pandemic, I would arrange for the loveliest florist in Spain (I am biased) to deliver some joy in the form of flower displays – always pink, full of roses, sometimes freesias, and absolutely no lilies!

My mum and I had our differences, especially during the time of my cancer diagnosis, surgery, and treatment, but over the last five years we gained a mutual respect which I hold dear. In February 2022, I was able to honour my mum by reading her eulogy, and my sister and I made sure there was a beautiful service to celebrate Mum's life. I really don't know how we managed it, as in Spain the funeral usually takes place within two days. We managed, though, to delay it by one day, enabling some family to travel to Spain.

There were beautiful flowers to honour her and that we knew she would have loved. And we toasted Mum with Cava and bottles of San Miguel, and platters of sandwiches. The sandwiches were a flashback to a time when my parents ran their local pub and sandwiches had to be cut in a particular way, decorated with salad leaves, cucumber (in very thin slices) and tomatoes, and served on huge silver platters.

We made sure we shared some of her life experiences and toasted Mum as she would have liked. At 17, she travelled by herself to Livorno in Italy to take up the role of nanny to two Italian children, so she had been a brave lady from an early age, and it was an experience she vividly remembered.

Photographs of Mum with her family were displayed with pride for all to see. For me, the most beautiful were of Mum in 1961, when she married my stepdad John for the first time. Mum was positively glowing in those amazing black and white photos. Their love for each other never died, and although they parted, they remarried in the early 1990s.

I imagine you are wondering how there could be a blessing in the loss of Mum. But I took care of her, and we shared laughter and tears. By honouring her life, I have been reminded of what a life well lived looks like. I intend to live my life with strength and love, as my mum did, even through the most challenging of times. And I am definitely going to wear more colourful clothes!

Inspirational Insight

Some of the positive steps I took to move forward with my life...

included staying positive and being incredibly grateful to be alive. I learned to honour how I truly feel, and to be open to learning new skills. In my situation, I looked at diverse ways to aid my own healing journey, to have something to aim for – an event or a goal. I also learned to understand that asking for and accepting help when I needed it, would help me and the lovely person helping me.

If you are going through any similar challenges right now, I absolutely want you to know...

that there is support, help, and healing available to you. There is light at the end of what can seem the darkest tunnel.

I wish I had known...

that I would find the courage and strength to pick myself up repeatedly after different challenges, and that each of these would make me stronger, more determined, and more resilient than I could ever have thought possible. I am immensely grateful for so many blessings in my life. I have a plaque on my desk which reads: "You are braver than you believe, stronger than you seem, and smarter than you think."

I wish I had realised much earlier in my life that I am the author of my own life.

I was Beautifully Broken.

I am now resilient, strong, and thriving.

Dedication

I dedicate this chapter to my beautiful daughters, Sarah and Georgina, and my amazing granddaughter, Sophie. You are my reason to be here and to continue to show up every day. My love for you is eternal.

I have been loved and supported by my family and friends over the years and would not be here without it, along with the support of the amazing teams at New Cross Hospital and Russells Hall.

My healing friends have guided me and supported me through good and bad times, and for this I am so grateful.

And finally, I dedicate this chapter to my amazing Mum, who lived a good life but endured so much, and who sadly died earlier this year. Always in my thoughts and forever in my heart. I love and miss you xxxxx

About the Author

Kate, who lives in Shropshire, has been described as loving, kind, strong, compassionate, and resilient. An authentic, humble, and brave warrior. Kate's precious family, friends, and fellow practitioners, are what make up her world. And she has a passion for complementary therapies, sharing her knowledge and skills in many different ways.

Being in nature is key, and particularly enjoying the beautiful Shropshire countryside with her little dog, Dottie.

Kate has been on an enlightening journey which has culminated in her becoming an aromatherapist, Reiki Master, Infinite Energy Healer, and author.

Kate's mission is to be a beacon of light and to inspire others on their journey.

Connect with Kate

www.scattergoodtherapies.com

Kate@scattergoodtherapies.com

Instagram: katefernandez2913

00447305499140

She Was There All Along!

Jacqueline Kent

What the fuck just happened to my life?
This was a text I sent about 2am, on a night I will never forget, in December 2014. An evening that had started just hours before, with me heading out to a fancy-dress party nearby dressed as Minnie Mouse, ended with me pinned to a wall by my throat by Mickey Mouse and fighting for my life! Sounds like a TV drama, doesn't it? It felt as though I was watching one from a distance.

I should have called the police as he drove away, leaving me in shock. And for a split second I thought to myself, *Shop him. Get him arrested for drunk driving, and take back what's left of your life.* But I didn't.

You might be wondering why not. But this life I lived felt an impossible juggling act of 'damned if I do, damned if I don't'. I was always worrying what effect my – yes, I held myself responsible for this mayhem in my life – actions might have on others, so I didn't make that call. Instead, I reached out to my best friend, who was beside herself with worry about me. She had been for a long time, in fact.

I gave myself such a hard time, wondering what I had done to make him behave like that, and it wasn't the first time I'd been made to feel that way.

As I went back over the events of that evening, I just found myself even more confused. My head was spinning, and I was in a state of shock. Automatic pilot soon kicked in, as it does when you're a mum, somehow still believing this was my mess to clear up. I collected our son, who thankfully remained blissfully unaware, and attempted to work out what would happen next. As things took a turn for the worse, and it was just a matter of hours before –safely in the company of a dear friend – I was being interviewed by the police.

I was stunned. What did this mean? It was a 'severe domestic violence incident', by their evaluation, because I could have lost my life. And I now had important decisions to make about things I never dreamed would be part of my world. I had always told myself: 'No-one ever lays a finger on me, or they'll be out the door.'

But everyone deserves a second chance. Right? This is where I came to an understanding some years later that I truly had reached a fork in the road, yet it felt like I still had work to do. I couldn't just give up now. Could I?

From that point on, I found myself crumbling. I was a shell of the woman I thought I was – the self-doubt, lack of self-worth, no self-esteem, a life completely void of any feelgood factor, had been my reality in the months and years before this incident. Oh, I looked happy enough on the outside. I had a husband, happy kids, my own business. But when I look back now, I realise I was living a lie.

Was it possible that this incident could lead the way to a deeper understanding? We could seek help and maybe move forward as a family, and everything would be alright? I truly felt as though I had an angel on one shoulder and a devil on the other. Each had a case to argue for and against, but I wasn't sure which one to believe. And most importantly – I cannot stress how important or significant this was – I didn't trust myself.

Have you ever found yourself so unsure what to do for the best that you don't even know which way is up? It's one thing to read about something like this and 'know' what you would do, but it's a completely different thing to take action, especially when you feel you are drowning in a sea of impossible despair.

During the difficult months that followed, I struggled to recognise myself. Who was this woman who put her marriage, her 'foundations', above what she knew to be true? Who was this woman that told those around her what she knew they wanted to hear, and then did the exact opposite. berating herself for making choices which she would be furious about, had this been about anyone else. Who was this emotional wreck of a woman who welled up instantly at songs that reminded her of the life she thought she knew?

This self-destructive path was to ripple out among my friends and family. Some didn't know how to express their deep concern for my well-being. So, they kept quiet. Others said if it was them, they would make this decision or that decision. But it's easy to say when it's not you.

And as for the family I was struggling so hard to hold together – I didn't know what I was doing this for any more. The atmosphere at home could be cut with a knife. Everyone knew the truth about what had brought me to that point, but I couldn't see – I chose not to see it. I repeated the story that 'it was for us'.

Almost 18 months later, another incident – not me at risk this time – found the police and social services back at my front door.

"If I could bottle the perfect parent and present her to you, it would be this woman." I've never forgotten that character witness statement from our local school.

Maybe it was going to be okay. As the household dynamic shifted once more, this time I found myself with a little more space to breathe, to think about what I needed. I had time to process some of these emotions that I'd stored inside for so long, unable to truly feel who I was inside.

But she was there all along.

And that brings me to a session with my life coach in August 2016. Now it gets really good!

By that time, I'd realised something needed to change desperately and I couldn't keep living like this. My life was just going to keep repeating the same patterns, and deep down I knew that. So, when I started the session with this coach, she began the conversation with six little words: "Tell me about your life today."

I just laughed. Imagine feeling so terrible about the shape of your life – and everything in it – that all you can do is laugh about it. Not because it's funny, but because it's bloody tragic.

I couldn't even find the words. I began to describe how I was where I had come to be, and I can so clearly remember her saying to me, "Think about what you want. Think about how you want to feel when you wake up every morning. Make choices to support that."

I could feel this enormous question mark over my head. *What does she think she's talking about? Could that possibly be a thing?* The situation in my home life was impossible. *How could thinking about what I needed or putting myself first help anybody?* Against my better judgement, though, I took her advice. I'd paid her to help me, and because I needed answers. I was desperate for someone to tell me what to do. So, why not her?

And so it began.

It started with really finding a way to the emotional state that I wanted, a feeling that I wanted to evoke: some kind of joy. Fulfilment instead of utter despair would have been great for a start. And she talked me through how I was going to start achieving that. I couldn't quite believe what she was suggesting, but I did it anyway. And I remember the look on the faces of those who didn't understand why I was even making this choice.

I decided it was time not to care about other people; it was time to care about what I wanted and needed, above everybody else. Because if I didn't, where the hell was I going to end up? Another police visit? More drama? Another episode in the soap opera that had become my life – or worse? Enough was enough. You have to know when you have reached your 'enough is enough' moment – and I hope it doesn't look anything like this!

It was a matter of weeks before everything changed forever, as a result of taking the time to 'do the work'. But this time it was a change for the better.

I was feeling ready now. To close the door on the enormous chapter of my life that was my first marriage. I had to make this choice. It was finally time to accept that what had come about was what should have happened all those months before, but I just hadn't been strong enough then. Now I'd spent time investing in me, investing in my well-being, my future, my happiness, and understanding that it wasn't down to anybody else to make me feel happy. That was my turning point.

It was a beautiful sunny autumn day, and I clearly remember I'd had this conversation that had ended with me thinking I was finally going to be free. Could this be? I was ready to start doing things differently. And so, as I took my sons out into the fresh air, I made one decision – a really simple one that was going to set the scene for the rest of my life. It was time to make a change. All we did was go to a different park, somewhere we hadn't been before. But it was time to take new directions, time to stop repeating the same patterns.

It was time to make new choices.

And so began the first day of the rest of my life as a single parent – 26th of October, 2016.

When the clocks went back that weekend, I wanted to make every minute count, so I went online and booked a holiday for the following summer – four nights in the Isle of Wight, just me and my two youngest boys, with not a care in the world. It was the first time I had booked anything like that by myself – I felt so brave!

The months that followed were heavily invested in me. It was my time now. I deserved this. I wasn't going to have someone telling me who or how I should be, or feel, or show up, or do any bloody thing. This was my life. I knew that I had enough about me now to make good choices, when no longer influenced by people who didn't really have my best interests at heart. That was when it all changed.

But I really needed to heal, recover, and become new. I needed to dig a little deeper and find and understand the reasons why I'd kept repeating this unhealthy pattern of poor choices, unworthiness, missed opportunities. And I couldn't do that if I was always considering the effect on anyone else. I'm not talking about my sons here. They would always be top of my priority list. But at the same time, if everything about looking after them — financially supporting them, caring for them, helping them grow into responsible young men — while dealing with everything that comes as being a mum and a carer on a day-to-day basis was all coming down to me, then how could I not think about looking after myself better, being healthier, being happier?

I started by indulging myself in a gym membership that gave me time and space to relax in a spa whenever I wanted. I took every opportunity I had when there was no-one else to look after. And I loved that time; it really felt like I was soothing my soul. I began meditating, and joined a group healing programme which found me receiving distance reiki healing every week. I immersed myself in this journey of inner and outer healing and finding my way to harmonious happiness — for me. And I could not be clearer that this is what it was about.

This would be the key which unlocked everything. If I didn't learn to love myself, for me, I would never feel truly fulfilled or happy. So I started living my life in a way that had others watching in awe — they wanted to feel like I did. Those settling for second best, maybe unhappy in situations or relationships which had them feeling unfulfilled or unsatisfied, were perhaps a little envious of the way I was so free and had the world at my feet. But they were also inspired; I know that now. However, they would have to go on their own journey. I wasn't doing this to make others feel anything at all; it was about doing exactly what I needed.

I was positively glowing. Strangers in the street would pass comment about how bright I beamed, which always made me smile. I knew I'd got this.

I still felt I had so much work to do, though! The truth is, we aren't ever 'completed' – the nature of evolving is a constant work in progress. I had a business in the wedding industry at the time, so that became a positive focus for the future. I wanted the kind of business that truly supported me and my boys, though I still had a vision of being a writer in a room filled with books, when I would serve only the highest level of wedding stationery clients with 'less is more'. But something felt a little out of whack. I couldn't explain what, but by keeping focused on all of the good stuff, I trusted it would eventually find its own way.

I could do this now and I truly felt I was capable of anything. I didn't need a man. I know some of that was a result of seeing, almost from a distance now, what had happened to me and how little I thought of myself from being in a toxic relationship. But I was determined I would never let another person make me feel that way again. I spent time learning, growing, hanging out with friends, having fun, letting my hair down, and just being. Loving my life, exactly as it was.

Early in the summer of 2017, I went away by myself to start writing what I thought was going to be my first book – all about planning your wedding stationery. It seems funny to think about that now. And I clearly remember just how amused I was by the proprietor of the beautiful cottage I stayed in. "You're writing a book? That's so cool!" Followed by the question, "What, you're staying by yourself? You don't have *anyone* with you?" He later joked that if I returned the following year and was still single, he would make an honest woman of me. He was in his 70s, at least! But the idea that any man would make me happier than I already was just made me laugh even more! I was loving this time of just being me so much!

As I sit writing this, it's April 2022. So what on earth has happened to my life now?

In November last year, after several lockdowns due to Covid-19, postponing by a year, and almost three years in the planning, I married my soulmate, Bruce. Our meeting of minds in July 2017 was the next stage in my own personal journey. Finding him was like coming home – but I know for certain that our paths would never have crossed had I not worked long and hard to recognise and identify the woman I am today. We were fortunate enough to both be at the perfect place in our lives to recognise something so good that we would have been fools to ignore it. It was a piece of my puzzle I had never expected to find. My missing piece.

I've continued on my personal development journey, while reorganising my life to be exactly how I want it. No more chasing after wedding stationery clients; I put that business to bed in 2020. I took everything that happened that year as a sign that this path had run its course.

My working week now looks very different. I've published two of my own books, co-authored several others, and I focus on helping women at life's crossroads to find their own way. The Tuneless choir, who sang their hearts out at our wedding, are also significant in the work I do as the manager of our local branch. It makes people happy to sing like no-one is listening, and this is hugely important to me.

It hasn't been easy. Between me and Bruce, we have navigated a LOT of 'stuff' along the way. But each challenge has presented new opportunities for learning and, by peeling back layers, we have helped heal each other. And I truly believe this is where the magic happens.

There's still more work to do – there is always work to do. But in the past few months I have appeared in national newspapers sharing my story, on local TV talking about my work with the choir, and delivered wonderful crystal healing sessions, following my certification last year.

I LOVE helping women uncover who they truly want to be through my Happy Life Activation business – in a similar way to how I started my own journey. Now I have a really lovely, engaged community of women who feel inspired by my caterpillar-butterfly metamorphosis (I can say that with real confidence). I BELIEVE in who I am becoming – and this is a huge deal for me, as I am living an authentic life at last. I also work alongside Cassandra Farren, helping heart-led authors to share their story and bring their journeys to life. And next month I will be speaking on stage for the first time.

It's so exciting to see what the future has in store every single day – new adventures are waiting to unfold. I can't wait!

Inspirational Insight

Some of the positive steps I took to move forward with my life were...

learning that it was absolutely 100% okay to put me first. It was essential, in fact. Understanding this and believing it, though, were quite different. Yet as pieces of my life slowly started to shift, I found myself knowing that I had done the right thing – for the greater good of all. And so will you.

I invested in myself and gave myself time and space to adapt. I stopped expecting so much of myself all of the time, and allowed myself room to breathe. My healing journey began with what felt right for me – a little time out once a week was just perfect to begin with, and it was enough. It also sent out a strong message to the universe that I understood I truly mattered, at last. I invested my time, my energy, and my commitment, to a new way of being. I gradually reassessed my trusted circle, got clear on who was in my life to make it better, and focused on only those people. I call them my cheerleaders.

If you are going through any similar challenges, I want you to know...

you are not alone. It won't feel like this forever. This icky part of your life is just a phase – and yes, I know you probably don't want to believe that.

But if you look around, you will find perfect examples of people who have come through these trials and survived, eventually coming out stronger. You ARE going to find happiness, but it starts within you. Try not to seek external validation from others; they don't have the answers. Trust that you are enough, just as you are – and you will slowly find your way to the biggest, brightest, boldest version of you, one you didn't even realise existed. But she was there all along.

I wish I had known...

that taking better care of my needs wasn't selfish. It was the key to unlocking everything.

I wish I'd known it was completely okay to stop worrying about how my actions affected everyone around me, when they worried so little how I was doing. I wish I hadn't paid so much attention to life-sapping drains who 'borrowed' my power, until that day I found myself running on empty, and they weren't around to help top me back up again.

If I had opened my eyes to possibilities, instead of believing that I had to be everything to everyone, I might have found solutions much faster.

I wish I'd known that by being more honest with myself I would find a way to step more fully into being – much quicker than I actually did. Although everything happened with divine timing, in the end.

I was Beautifully Broken.

I am now a Powerhouse of a Woman, one who sets an example to others of just what's possible. Each day I shine brighter and bolder than the day before. I've regained my inner strength and am proud of who I have become. This is a gift, and I intend to share it far and wide.

Dedication

Jacqueline dedicates this chapter to all those women who have found themselves stuck at life's crossroads with no idea how they can ever move forward. She wants you all to know that you can change direction at any time, safely and with support, and that no challenge is too great. She knows you are amazing beings who are ready to find yourselves once more, and she looks forward to being inspired by your stories too, one day.

About the Author

Jacqueline has been described as a sparkling soul who lights up the room when she enters – her energy is captivating!

A natural writer, she is now the published author of two of her own books, plus numerous collaboration titles. When she isn't writing, she loves to be creative, enjoying time with her family and her soulmate Bruce. Maybe you will find them singing, dancing, or perhaps just 'being', with family time also very high on her list. She loves to inspire others with her journey, sharing the lessons and light bulb moments.

Her typical day consists of writing, helping women on their journey, and constantly learning new modalities to improve – and she does this in just such a way that you can't help but pay attention.

Jacqueline's mission, and her glass half-full kind of attitude, aims to inspire a generation of women to believe in themselves so they can move from a muddled, midlife 'meh' to finding a marvellous, magnificent Me (she was there all along!).

Connect with Jacqueline

Visit her website: www.jacquelinekent.co.uk

Join her mailing list here: bit.ly/gentlebumkick

Join her Facebook group at www.facebook.com/groups/jkcfreegroup

Or Instagram www.instagram.com/jacquelinekentofficial

Jacqueline has published two books – *Onward and Upward* (under her maiden name, Jacqueline Rogerson) and *You've Got This!* (Jacqueline Kent) – both are available on Amazon.

Becoming Amy...

Amy Fleckney

There I was on the floor at nine months pregnant, doing a pedicure for a friend just to create a little bit of money for myself. All my thoughts were based on a bigger and better life to come for me. I was in a position where I didn't really have my own money and was controlled financially within my relationship.

Everything I ever wanted in my head was always bigger, better, and more! Have you ever had that feeling where you can just see it in your mind, but your reality doesn't quite match?

I was pregnant with my second child, and in my attempt to stay sane all I could think about was that I had to keep going. My mental health was in tatters. My children's father was all I knew at this time. I had moved away to be with him and, despite the challenges, I still had hope that we were creating a better life and a family together. I have to say, when our relationship was good, it was amazing, but when it was bad... it was dark.

The dark times included behaviour that was controlling, mentally abusive, and toxic. This happened a lot. My home life wasn't the perfect family life I had dreamt of, and I was desperately trying to just keep going to the end of this pregnancy to meet my baby.

I was already mum to a beautiful daughter, but I don't feel anyone can prepare you for motherhood, especially when having children was never in your original life plan. Growing up, I had friends who just wanted to have children, but I'd never felt like that. I wanted to be a wife – marriage was so important to me – and I wanted success, enough money to be comfortable, and to be known for changing lives.

It sounds extreme when I say it out loud like that, but I used to imagine during my school years that somehow Amy Fleckney would become someone. I speak about her like she isn't me, but at that time when I was sitting on the floor at someone's feet, waiting for my baby to arrive, I had lost who I was or what I wanted for me and my life going forward. I just existed in the long days of walking on eggshells, wondering who my partner would decide to be that day. He could be so many different people in one, and I spent many long nights lying in my daughter's bed, because I knew I was safe there from his crazy, drunk, abusive behaviour.

I would let tears silently roll down my cheeks as I lay there holding my breath, just waiting for things to go silent so that I knew he had passed out asleep. And I would watch my little girl sleep, and thank her repeatedly for keeping me alive. She was my purpose, my reason, and the air that I could breathe.

At one point, I remember things got so torturous that I begged my mum to take me to a hospital and put me to sleep, just so it would all stop. By this I mean the torture of my own mind being taken over by someone else. He would make decisions for me, talk for me, tell me how to cook, how to clean, how to be a mum, how to be me…

I was obsessed with being the best mum I could be, and it was my only purpose for so long that my mental health was declining. Some days I would find myself biting the skin from around my nails till it bled, or wanting to pull my hair from my scalp just to stop my mind from feeling the fog.

I was 26 years old with a little girl and a new baby on the way. Surely life wasn't supposed to be this hard?

When my son arrived, I felt so lucky! Never in my wildest dreams during my pregnancy did I ever believe I would be fortunate enough to be a mum to a girl and a boy! As my beautiful baby boy was placed into my arms, his father was overjoyed to have a son – I had given him the boy his family longed for.

That was the moment when I believed things would change. He would make better choices, the drinking would stop, and maybe he would have a complete turnaround in his attitude towards me.

But no, it didn't. In fact, the early years of my son's life are a blur to me. Even now, when I attempt to dig deep for the memories, they aren't there. I remember surviving the days, but I don't remember him walking, talking, or any of the usual milestones, because things just got harder. I was simply in survival mode.

By the time my son was four months old, I knew my time was up and I had to leave their dad. I didn't leave because I didn't love him, and I wasn't sure why I did love him any more, but I had been convinced I wasn't worthy of love, respect, and anything better than what life had given me, and I was so grateful for my children that I wondered why I should need or want more. The truth was, I didn't know who I was any more… I didn't know what I enjoyed doing, my interests, or even what I wanted to eat! I had been controlled for so long, and all I was good at was bringing up my kids in the best way I could.

It was so painful for me to leave him, and it took me many attempts to actually go. All that ran through my head was how was I going to live without him. You might be wondering why I would want to live with him, but when you have been conditioned to become dependent on someone, the thought of flying solo is absolutely terrifying!

I kept giving myself deadlines: after Christmas I'll go; after the baby's christening I'll go; tomorrow I'll go. It was always tomorrow…

As I struggled, he kept using my mental health battle against me, telling me I was mad, that I wasn't fit to be a mum, and that I would ultimately lose my children because I wasn't stable enough to look after them.

Looking back now, I know this would never happen. My doctor at the time looked at me with such sad eyes when I went to him for help but begged him not to give me medication because I would lose my children. He knew I had been brainwashed into believing this, but at the time the fog was becoming thicker in my mind and clarity was becoming lost. The doctor was aware of my volatile relationship, as a few years previously he had prescribed me antibiotics for a human bite on my arm. When people say they have a good doctor, I was definitely fortunate enough to have one. He never once pushed me to share information I didn't want to talk about, and he trusted that I had never lost my mind. He would always say, "You're a clever girl, Amy, don't ever give up. You can be anything!" I used to come out of his appointments smiling and remembering my hopes and dreams, and the fog always seemed a little clearer each time I left.

He reassured me I would never lose my children for asking for help for my mental health. And I can honestly say he played a massive role in saving me and for reminding me of my worth. When I left the children's father, my self-worth was on the floor, and I felt like I would never achieve anything. I almost accepted that life would be one big tough road. and that I would never really be anyone – and definitely not the Amy Fleckney I had imagined growing up.

As a single mum of two young kids, being a beauty therapist and doing the odd set of nails and eyebrows wasn't going to give me the life I had once visualised in my mind. But I was grateful I had something to keep me going other than being a mum, and it helped to keep a roof over our heads and food on the table. That in itself was such a challenge, whilst keeping my shit together mentally and dealing with a feral ex who was still not letting go and causing havoc.

We all knew he wasn't going to let me walk away quietly, but I had no idea how I was going to change things. I faced a constant battle of no money, no fuel, and trying to do nice things for the kids whilst deciding should I pay the bills or do I eat!

Being a single mum isn't the fun-fuelled life some might think, but I wear my single parent badge with pride. We are a rare breed with incredible strength, and you have to be in that situation to really understand it. Often, I would wonder if I'd messed everything up for my kids by leaving their dad. But I knew that I couldn't have continued to raise them in that toxic environment. They deserved so much better, and it was down to me to make sure they had better.

The smile on my face became so easy to fake that even I believed I was happy on some days! But I became really unwell as the stress took over my body, and I suffered from stomach pains and frequent chest infections as I struggled to keep going. I knew I had no choice but to fight on, as I had two little people depending on me. But sometimes I wondered if I'd ever sleep at night again.

Two years after I left the children's dad, I had lost two houses and was now living in a mobile home, in a lorry yard. It was on private land, and it created distance from my ex and gave me a chance to breathe, get well, and attempt to start my life again as I neared my 30th birthday. My son was by then two and my daughter seven, and they loved the freedom of being able to run free. I guess to them it was one big holiday living in a caravan.

My original intention was to stay at the caravan for six months, but three years later we were still there, with people beside me who cared for and looked out for us, and finally the fog started to lift.

I could see my visions again in my mind, just as I had years before when I lay in my daughter's bed all those nights, or sitting on the floor doing a pedicure, or during my school days when I had the idea of Amy Fleckney being a name to be proud of.

I was visualising…

The caravan was quiet and safe. When the kids were asleep, I would often sit on my outside step and gaze up at the stars shining so brightly, and reconnect with my spiritual side. All my life I had what some would call a gift. My earliest experience of being able to connect to spirit was when I was eight years old, so it was always just who I was. But over the years I had parked or ignored it as I lost myself to abuse.

Now, though, my psychic intuition began to come back, and I started to rekindle my interest in crystal healing.

Losing my nan many years before had left a huge hole in my heart. But during my time at the caravan, I started to feel her presence again from the spirit world. It had been there the whole time. I owe spirit so much, and my promise now to them is to always work to the best of my abilities to make sure their messages get to earth clearly and accurately.

In my second year in the caravan, I managed to come off medication for my depression, and although I wasn't financially stable, my mindset was slowly starting to move into a more positive space.

By the end of the third year, I made the decision to move to a new town with the opportunity for my children to go to new schools and to live in a house again. I'm not going to lie, the responsibility of this was tough going, but it was a move I had to make for them.

I was still struggling financially in a new home and new town, and still in awe of businesswomen around me, but I was fortunate enough to have some incredible role models in my life, including friends and their parents. In particular, I always loved being around the energy of my best friend Vicky and her mum. Vicky's mum was, and still is, a successful and strong businesswoman, and I would hang on her every word, like a sponge soaking up all her knowledge as I listened to her talk about her big plans and her ownership of life. It was totally inspiring. I wanted to be her!

Then, just like that, there was an opportunity for me to start doing spiritual readings for people. I was asked to do a couple for a friend who had become unwell and couldn't manage her workload. They were all done online, so there was no scary face-to-face stuff to throw me. I did them and smashed it!

I enjoyed the experience and loved the energy I created with clients. When my Nan died, no-one had been able to fill the dark space left in my heart, but now I felt the work I was doing exactly that for other people. With my ability to connect to spirit, I was able to bring those loved ones to earth and provide comfort, giving them the message from their loved ones to move forward with their lives.

I shocked myself every time I did a reading with the accuracy and clarity I was able to offer, and was really hard on myself to get it right and be the best I could be. This hasn't changed!

Slowly I began to see in my mind that my life was going to change. I had something unique that could not only change the lives of others, but it was also going to change mine and the kids by giving us stability. Was I finally going to be able to pay the bills, eat, and sleep at night again? I remember thinking that I could actually make something of this.

And so I did. I started to believe... and this is when shit gets real. I believed in myself and my vision!

I cared about people enough to share my ability to connect to their loved ones and to make this into a business. And one thing that people know who come into my online community is that I care, or what I would usually say is: I give a shit.

No-one is just a client; no-one is just a number. Just like the doctor who cared about me

enough to tell me I could do anything, I genuinely care!

Despite the fact that my ex didn't support my children and wasn't around much, financially, things started to get easier. I didn't have time to wallow in self-pity, so from then on, my visions become clearer, and I started to feel like someone again.

I was able to start living, and not just existing in the pain of the past and the fog of my mental health, which I still struggled with. I decided to invest in having Unconscious Mind Therapy (UMT) to help me manage things better, as the last thing I wanted was my business to suffer because I was unwell. How could I help heal others if I couldn't heal myself?

Unconscious Mind Therapy is a productive talking therapy that aims to resolve the problem that's holding you back in your life, rather than focusing directly on the problem. Unlike most therapies that often take months, if not years, to see improvement, UMT results are instantaneous. You can often feel the positive effect from the very first session!

And I did! It changed my whole way of thinking. Although I had the foundations of placing the right thought into my mind to become the reality in my hand, I never knew the depth of the power of my own thought process until then!

UMT focuses on the recovery rather than the content of the issue that is blocking your journey in your life, preventing you from moving forward and reaching your full potential.

It can help you change past thoughts, feelings, limiting beliefs, and patterns, and give you an incredible mindset to create the vision to be happy, focused, and in control.

So, from my first and only session of UMT, my life changed. I was becoming the businesswoman I had been in awe of with Vicky's mum. Someone my children could be proud of, and who was able to provide for them fully, with no fear or doubt. I could even start buying them dessert!

So much has happened since I decided to take control in my life, and my business has gone from strength to strength. I never give up, I never stop, and my desire to make my business the best means it is my second love, after my children.

And two years after my own session as a client, I found myself sitting at the UMT Academy, training to become a therapist!

So never forget: if you can think it, you can be it. If I can do it, so can you!

By creating a growing online following all over the world, to standing on a stage of over 100 people during my solo LIVE mediumship show, and supporting people to live a life they love, I was becoming Amy Fleckney, international psychic medium & Unconscious Mind Therapist.

And this was just the start...

To be continued!

Inspirational Insight

Some of the positive steps I took to move forward with my life were...

to not feel ashamed to ask for help. It's totally ok to need support and guidance, whether that be from friends or a professional.

It's not a sign of weakness; it's a sign of your strength and integrity to want better in life for yourself and the special people around you.

If you are going through any similar challenges, I want you to know...

nothing is impossible, nothing is out of reach, and dreams do become reality.

When people say you can't, prove them wrong. Because, trust me, you can!

Finding a home in your heart that will always keep you safe, a secure place that makes you realise how loved you are, will intuitively guide you to where you need and deserve to be.

In my case, it was my children.

We all have a gut feeling… trust it, and never let anyone take your power away. Live life on your terms, without fear or doubt. At times it may feel relentless, and it might not be easy, but I can promise you it will be worth it…

I wished I had known...

the power of the mind and how creating a vision, a thought, and a feeling, really does become your reality.

I learned to place the correct information into my brain and focus on what I really wanted for my life and how I saw it in my mind, rather than repetitive thoughts of what I didn't want.

Visualising is the key to creating a better life, and it all starts with you in your thoughts.

I found the switch in my hand to turn the light back on... I just didn't realise I was holding it the whole time.

Little did I know my ability to connect to spirit would support me and my children to a better life, I would be helping others to heal, and I'd become the businesswoman I had visualised becoming. It was inside of me the whole time.

I was Beautifully Broken.

I am now... free to be me.

Dedication

Jasmine,

You taught me to be the person I want to be. You saved me & you made me.

My daughter, my mini me, my everything. X

About the Author

Amy (with the long red hair), who lives in Essex, England, is well known as a fighting spirit and an incredibly hard worker.

She has been described as fiercely loyal, kind, and someone with their feet firmly flat on the ground.

She can usually be found working long hours as a renowned psychic medium and Unconscious Mind Therapist, who is committed to her clients and working with spirit, whilst simultaneously juggling the joys of being a full-time mother to her three beautiful children and life with her partner Joe.

Despite the hardships she has faced, she has always remained sedulous, and now finds herself with a growing following in the UK, America, and Australia, including celebrity clients, and continuing her journey as a stage platform medium.

A full encounter of her full story and all the details of the fascinating, and at times heart-breaking, chapters of her life can be found in her upcoming book, due to be released late 2022.

In the free time she has, she enjoys spending it with her parents and her close friends.

Amy's goal is to help as many people as possible to live a life they love, to give hope, to heal grief, and to provide for her children.

Connect with Amy

Website- www.amyfleckneymediumship.co.uk

Instagram- amyfleckneymedium

Email - info@amyfleckneymediumship.co.uk

Facebook Group – Amy's psychic mediumship reviews & more

A Spectrum of Solutions

Jillian Forster

Welcome to my chapter on my story. It's not the whole story, and I walked into this part of my life with quite different expectations.

My life had turned over a page, and everything was fresh and full of promise. When I was 40 years old, my first husband and I divorced, without children. Although we did try to produce offspring, it didn't happen. It was a marriage I had not been present in for some time, though we were a sociable couple on the face of things. But for me there was no spark. I had married a friend rather than a life partner.

Enter my second husband, who swept me off my feet, wrote me love letters, poetry, and showed me love that I had only thought of in wilder moments! I was vibrant with new energy, new love, and new possibilities. Within the space of two years, one marriage had ended and another began.

We started married life living in the Emirates. It was fast-paced; he worked long hours, while I had two jobs, daytime and evening. There was always plenty of socialising, too. Clubs, wild desert trips, beaches, and five-star restaurants, and I learnt golf. I loved it all. Within a year, I was pregnant, just as that contract ended and we moved, with our Himalayan colourpoint cat, to Saudi Arabia.

Being pregnant at 42 somewhat astonished me, but I took it all as being meant to be. I was in good health and accepting of it all.

My son was born in the UK, as I wanted my parents' support around the time of the birth. My husband worked long hours, as did most ex-pats. Also, my baby was heading into the world bottom-first, and I was certain I'd need a Caesarean.

Going to live at my parents' house, even temporarily, was odd. I had left home at 18 years of age to start student nurse training. As a teenager, I had been unhappy at home and felt very much the black sheep of the family. I was an independent sort, with my own ideas and opinions, young as I was. I loved to play both classical and rock music very loudly. An avid reader, I went through whole collections of authors I liked.

My family didn't discuss much, nor were they open to listen. Life had been bland at home. I grew up feeling that I had a purpose in life, but didn't know what.

So, I was right about the Caesarean; I opted for a spinal anaesthetic, as I wanted to hear my baby's first cry. I somehow knew I was having a boy, and along he came at 39 weeks pregnancy, in the same hospital where I had trained.

My son was handed to me, wrapped up, and squalling lustily; he did not want to be born just yet. He opened his eyes and we stared at each other. I took a sharp intake of breath. His deep brown eyes searched into my hazel ones with the clarity of a wise old sage; and at that moment, I felt I knew him totally.

Being a midwife did not prepare me for how strong the maternal bond is. Merely saying I loved my baby didn't come close. Gorgeous little man! How could I have waited this long to be a mum? My husband was delighted. Meanwhile, my whole system geared towards being a mother, and hormones raced through me. I had the 'four-day blues' when I was a blubbering wreck and anything made me cry, even peeling a banana. At 40 + and always being in charge of my life, I was taken over by an unexpected level of raw emotions.

My son was a demanding feeder and didn't sleep, so I was a tired mum. When he was four months old, I went back to work, teaching English at an International School. The schools there had free workplace nurseries, as most of the female staff had young children. When my son needed feeding, they fetched me, and afterwards I returned to teaching. It worked fine, though the sleep deprivation was hard. After a few months, I got a job at the local International School, and didn't have so much travelling time.

My son was thriving and passed all his first-year milestones, but was oh so active. No crawling; he got up and walked. Sleeping for longer than two hours was rare. The first time he slept a full five hours, I woke up in a panic, thinking he must have died in the night. He kept me on my toes, continually demanding breast feeding, and wanting deep hugs. Knowing what I do now about sensory dysfunction, I realise that he had several issues around proprioceptive, auditory, and visual senses.

And then, the period from 18 months to 2 years saw regression. Skills were lost. Speech and language went. He was only interested socially in me. He dropped food items from his diet so that he would only eat about five items by the age of three years. Toilet training was sporadic.

I became increasingly concerned, not least because my son was to start at the school nursery soon, and they would accept only toilet-trained children. So, while my gorgeous boy and I had a close relationship, he was steadily withdrawing. I asked myself why, what was going on, suspecting a communication disorder.

The nursery school teacher was a blunt South African lady, who looked at him and shook her head, muttering. The school openly said they couldn't support any child with special needs. At his third birthday, he had no speech; when I brought the birthday cake in, he jumped up and down, with a lot of hand-flapping. *Right*, I said to myself, *it's time to go home and sort this out.*

This is essentially my story, in that it's life as I experienced it. My son might tell quite a different tale. Others in my life might see circumstances differently, but it doesn't matter, as this is about me. And my experience is not an invitation to a pity party; I am not playing the sympathy card. This is about what emerged from the chaos of each life-changing step on this part of my journey, and how it became an opportunity for me to grow and find out what kind of person I am. I learnt what my boundaries are, and why they're important. Self-care was essential to keep myself sane and functioning at a moment's notice.

I was on high alert for years; battle-ready for every situation from meltdowns to multi-disciplinary teams' meetings, from doctors to support services, from unsolicited advice from strangers ('what he needs is a good slap') to being totally isolated. I dropped all judgement and blame, which I saw as a waste of time and energy. And I learnt that I liked myself. I was a pretty good sort of woman, and as a mum I sought solutions that would work for us, no matter what objections the nay-sayers came out with. But it took me a while to get to this happier state.

I left my Saudi home, my job, my husband, and my friends, and took my three-year-old son to the UK. We had bought a small house in a town where I knew no-one, only because it was near lovely sandy beaches and the scorching Saudi summer months were to be avoided. Our summer home was only half an hour's drive from my parents' house, and my mum was excited about her newest grandson being there. She did not see any of his difficulties. He actually related quite well with Grandma, who was smiley, expressive, and would watch and encourage him.

Autism was firmly in my mind by now, and like most parents, I started my own research as soon as we got a home computer set up.

With my 'health professional hat' on, I mapped out, in my head, an idea of how the diagnostic process would go. I would register with a local GP practice, make an appointment to see the doctor, and express my concerns. I expected an assessment of the four fields of development, like I was used to as a Health Visitor. I knew he'd fail in two of these fields. Then I expected a referral along a diagnostic pathway, where my son would be assessed and a plan put in place, which would be monitored and evaluated at appropriate intervals by suitably trained personnel. I had recently been a teacher responsible for improving the academic level of English at an International School, and had seen children from all kinds of language and cultures. I had a standardised test that I'd apply, then make individual programmes from the test results. So I thought a health pathway would be similar.

How optimistic was I for my son's diagnostic process and the ensuing years!

Services did not always do what they said they did, nor were they what they claimed to be. Sometimes they were the complete opposite. It was confusing. I had been a health service provider, and now I was a service user; it was a totally different matter to navigate the service provision. I learnt that many people we saw in health liked to fit my son into a box, based on their own expertise and the resources available to them. If they had no resources, it was my problem. We fell down a lot of gaps in services.

So, despite having lost most of his speech and language, my son wasn't referred to a Speech and Language therapist at all before starting school. I paid for a private assessment, but at the time couldn't afford weekly sessions, so I looked at her assessment and worked on my own with him. I did a lot of talking, in simple language and always in context. I explained everything in our world. How the vacuum worked by plugging it in; all the plants, rocks, and everything we saw and heard; the weather; how to make toast; what was in the shops. I talked to this little boy who rarely replied, but I knew he was taking it all in. I was busy all the time.

Then, one night I woke up in a cold sweat. The house was quiet, but my mind raced with a toxic cocktail of doubts, blame, grief, and guilt. My solar plexus felt like there was a hand on my stomach, twisting and wringing out my gut muscles. I was nauseous to the core of my being, and my head pounded. In the darkness of night, I looked into my own darkness.

Is my son's situation my fault? Have I failed him? Something I did, or didn't do? I have been trusted with a beautiful son, to bring him up, and cherish him, to show him the world. And now he is struggling in ways I could not have imagined. Language disappearing; speech repetitive; becoming increasingly fussy with food; behaving oddly with objects, like wanting to tip everything over and watch it fall, repeatedly; no progress with toilet training.

And the awful thing was, I didn't know what to do. I was his mum. I was losing my son. I was scared.

My life had been starting anew and all mapped out to my satisfaction, with my son being the icing on the cake. But now, I'd lost my job, my house and friends in Saudi, and my husband wasn't with me to help. I dived head first into victim mode: WHY ME? Why was this happening to me?

For hours that night, dark thoughts were my companions, twisting my head this way and that. When I got up at daylight and looked at my son, I had a rush of reassurance – goodness knows where from – and a flush of warmth. But it wasn't just because I loved him. I became conscious, for maybe the first time in years, of a spiritual strength holding me. I knew I could do a good job, though at the time I couldn't have known what was involved in being an autism parent.

I soon found out. There was a growing list of jobs adding to my parental role. With a special needs child, the support they need is broader than a typical child and carries on for far longer. There was much that my son couldn't cope with, because of sensory issues.

One day I was at a parents' seminar, and we all wrote down what we did for our children, on top of being a parent. *Deep intake of breath…* researcher, nutritionist, a range of therapists: occupational speech and language, behavioural, play and musical, sleep; physio, advocate, personal secretary (oh, all those endless reports to write), driver, hairdresser, chiropodist, personal shopper (for all sorts of sensory stuff), cleaner, garden designer, decorator, representative at all sorts of meetings, interviewer. I was a parent on a mission. As the saying goes, I thought I would have to teach my child about the world; it turned out that I had to teach the world about my child.

The diagnosis process followed swiftly, fortunately, perhaps because it was so obvious my son had delays. I remember being shown into a room with about four others: doctor, psychologist, medical student, nursery worker. They looked nervous and were hushed, as if about to tell me something awful that I didn't already know. The med student looked bored rigid; he had the same name as my son. I remember wondering if his mum was proud of him, as I was of mine.

Slight clearing of throats, and they put it to me; they thought my son was autistic. They were so serious I found it amusing. I'd already got used to the idea and was researching madly. I asked them what made them think this, and could it be anything else. I just wanted to know their thought processes. They looked sadly at me, and I could read their thoughts: *Poor mother, she's in denial.*

We had a referral to see a child psychiatrist after that and got the formal diagnosis. She handed me an out-of-date leaflet for the National Autistic Society; the old leaflet where there's a crying child and a jigsaw puzzle. Nothing about any local help. I was thoroughly dismayed. Eighteen months later, the same doctor told me that I was 'coping' with my son's autism, and she was discharging him from her clinic. 'Does that mean he's no longer autistic?' I asked, and, 'What about approaches such as a gluten-free diet?' She admitted she knew nothing about anything that might help. There was nothing in the mainstream that autism fitted into.

We were alone in uncharted seas, with no compass.

Just after my son's diagnosis, my mum suddenly collapsed and died, five days after my son's fourth birthday. She was only 69. I took photos at the birthday party, and Mum was not in one of them, even though she had been sitting at the table with all of us. My dad was distraught and plunged into a deep despair; he said he felt cheated. He was lost. We scraped together cash and bought a larger house, and Dad came to live with us. For a while I had a depressed diabetic dad, who found it hard to motivate himself to move, and an autistic youngster who couldn't keep still. They ate different food, enjoyed different things, but somehow rubbed along well enough.

Dad couldn't be left with my son, though, as he simply fell asleep at the drop of a hat. One day, he said he'd watch him while I had a snooze (I was bone-deep exhausted), and I woke to the sound of frantic banging on the front door from a neighbour at the back. My son had got out of an upstairs window and was balancing along the windowsill while Dad snoozed, pleasantly unaware.

There were years of relentless pressure and stress to find and implement therapies or approaches to help my son, and then maintain them. I started him on some supplements, which helped enormously, and thus began his nutritional regime that continues to this day. I found out about a summer camp that had an approach based on sensory and communication needs, and for the first time I met and spoke with therapists who understood his sensory profile. Oh joy, to have solutions to these issues that had mystified me. We started a behavioural programme, and his speech and language returned. The day he again called me 'Mummy', my heart burst with love to hear him. He voiced a name to the relationship we have, and I loved it.

Everything took planning, time, and all sorts of resources. I bought and made visual aids, play, and therapeutic items. An upstairs bedroom became a school room; my son couldn't cope with full-time school, and neither could they work with him. 'Experts' were often unable to teach my son. I had my own thoughts on that, but meanwhile I pressed on.

Offers of help from family and friends were not forthcoming. His father came home for a year, but it was not what he thought his life ought to be. I was 'blamed' for our son's issues. As soon as he could, he applied for a job and left us. I did not want the marriage to fall apart but could see it was hopeless and, within a few years, we were divorced. I remember reading at the time that 85% of marriages where there was an autistic child ended in divorce. We became just another of those clinical statistics.

There was progress, but it was exhausting me, and I had no respite at that time. I often felt sick with tiredness, wanting to sleep and never wake up. I was not depressed, merely weary to the core and needing a break. A local beach with stunning views over the Channel had a cliff road that we drove down many times. This was to be my escape for when I could take no more pressure. I would go over those cliffs. Wheeee... An exhilarating moment of flying, followed by oblivion. I didn't believe in a hell; I had always done my best. I would sleep blissfully forever.

However, there was a fly in the ointment of this course of action: my son. Who would care for him? He was the only reason I didn't leave this earth at the time. A short while later, the council moved the cliff road inland, erecting solid posts, so that driving over the cliff was impossible. It was my turn to feel cheated. Even though I rationalised that I couldn't leave my son, my plan had been thwarted!

Life improved. I was given four hours' respite weekly, then a budget to employ Personal Assistants for my son. I focussed more regularly on myself, discovering belly dance classes and Reiki. I learnt the necessity of nurturing myself physically and spiritually.

My story continues. I offer you a snapshot into our early autism world, but our road contained many other potholes and pitfalls. After several harrowing years, my son now lives supported by a consistent team of carers, in his own home.

There are two motivating factors in this world: love and fear. I am motivated by love, which is expansive, and seeks solutions; it nurtures and is compassionate. In environments where fear is present, there is no growth; the individual is stifled; the mind numbed; abuse is prevalent. I have seen it. I am always grateful for those who have come into my life with good hearts and honest smiles. I feel truly blessed.

Inspirational Insight

Some of the positive steps I took to move forward in my life were...

all around deciding priorities in my life, and installing healthy boundaries. Because of the time I needed to put into my son, and his therapies in particular, I had to rethink what my priorities were very early on. I had always been the strong one, there for others. Now it was me needing help, and it wasn't necessarily forthcoming from friends and family. I got the pruning shears and cut out the dead wood from my life. With great respect for all, I left any relationship that drained me. This became natural when I took to energy work on a daily basis. Because we are all energy and frequency, I came to see why some people left my life and others entered; we were an energetic match. I gained, rather than lost, a whole new tribe of the most wonderful people I've ever met.

If you are going through any similar challenges, I want you to know...

that you are worth any effort that you put into yourself. When you're under constant stress, there's no space to be a victim. 'Why me?' has to be worked out at a deep level. You learn that it's not happening TO you, it's happening FOR you. For your growth and learning as a human with a heart.

Neither can you be a martyr to your cause. Accept help; ask for it. There are kind people everywhere. It's hard enough without thinking that you are the only one who can do absolutely everything. I also want you to know that things change; nothing stays the same forever. You need to ensure that the change is in the direction that you want to see. Be proactive.

I wish I had known...

practical and health information. There are some measures I would have taken earlier, and some I would not have done. I don't blame myself, though. I did my best at all times with what knowledge and resources I had. I grieved for the son I'd thought I would have, and that is a natural process. I began to see that our social conditioning is very narrow, and that wandering from the prescribed life path of school, university, career, marriage, debt, etcetera, can open up a wonderful world of new thinking and possibilities. Doing one's own thing is liberating. It's not thinking outside the box; it's realising that there is no box. I learnt quickly, and had an open mind to new approaches, always mindful of their safety and efficacy. I wish I'd known my own power, and to be happy in trusting my intuition.

I was Beautifully Broken.

I am now wiser and an empowered feminine. I accept and go with the flow of life. I easily forgive, and release what no longer serves me, with love and gratitude for the lesson. I realise where I was stuck in my life and was lacking in purpose. I look forward to each day with love.

Dedication

To my son, who touched my soul from the first moment we met.

About the Author

Understandably, when Jillian's only child, a boy, was born in her early 40s, life was never going to be quite the same again. A complete change of circumstances threw Jillian's family life into a whirlwind of uncertainty when it became evident that her beautiful son was struggling with the basics of language, communication, and had severe sensory challenges. Jillian had previously trained as a nurse, midwife, health visitor, and teacher of English as an Additional Language. She used all her skills and experience in the ensuing years, searching for and implementing positive solutions when the given outlook was gloomy.

Jillian took over and developed a local autism support group, which she ran for 16 years, and which thrives to date, supporting hundreds in her local area. Over the years she organised activities, training for parents, clubs and holiday breaks, co-curated an autism art exhibition, was a guest speaker on local and national radio, wrote articles, and delivered presentations at carers' events, Cardiff University, and at the Senedd in Cardiff Bay.

Through being a parent carer, Jillian found unanticipated ways of relieving the relentless pressure of 24/7 care. She discovered a local belly dance class, and now teaches and performs. Jillian went on a school trip when her son was six years old, where she had a Reiki taster, and this began her Reiki path. Jillian became a Master Teacher/Practitioner, using the healing energy on herself and her son, as well as developing a practice. In the past five years, her path has included shamanic drumming, singing, and toning. This year, she became a Magdalene Priestess of the Rose. Jillian is currently working towards completing a Diploma in Naturopathic Nutrition.

Jillian says that being a parent carer made her realise how crucial it is to love and care for yourself, on all levels: physical, emotional, mental, and spiritual.

Connect with Jillian

Email: ForsterJauthor@hotmail.com

From Hope
to Healing

Lois Lane

We are not necessarily doubting that God will do the best for us. We are wondering how painful the best will be. - C.S. Lewis

It's November 2015. The dark is surrounding me, overwhelming me. I don't know where I am, and I'm scared, frustrated, and a little angry. Why am I here? Why is my body not functioning properly? You don't care about me enough to stop bad things from happening to me. You might let me die here on this dark, lonely road. My God, why have you forsaken me?

Months earlier, in January of that year, I had been in the house when my husband called from outside, "Lois! Come quick and see what Braelon is doing!"

Braelon, my grandson, was three years old at the time, and everything he did was, of course, amazing and adorable. I hurried outside and saw Braelon sitting on my husband's lap in the golf cart. Not knowing what he was going to do, I simply perched on the edge of the seat, and waited for him to honk the horn or some other cute thing. But his Pop-Pop said, "OK, Braelon!"

Braelon slid off his grandpa's lap and stood on the gas pedal.

What occurred next happened so fast, and the golf cart turned sharply. I remember lurching backwards, and before getting my balance, the golf cart turned quickly and I was lunging forward and sideways, out of the golf cart, landing face down on my forehead, on the hard ground. A body in motion stays in motion. Until it doesn't! It felt like I had slammed against concrete.

I remember thinking, *I'm going to die.* That's how bad the pain was. My whole body was sick, and my head felt like it was exploding. All I could do was say, "Don't touch me," and try to breathe. I thought if I moved, or was touched, I would break completely. It would be over. I was crying in pain and disbelief! Why had this happened? Again?

I'd suffered several head injuries before this. The first one I remember was in second grade, when I was pushed off the top of one of those old-fashioned ten-foot slides on the playground at recess. That was the beginning of dizzy spells and nosebleeds. But I also woke up in 'Prince Charming's' arms. Actually, it was a fourth grader carrying me into the school. But he looked like a hero to me.

My mom was told to meet us at the hospital, but that I was okay. She took one look at me and broke down crying. My face was really swollen. She was not happy at the disinformation, to say the least, and was worried about what this meant for me and the future… and thus it began.

And here I was again. Lying on the ground. Only this time, I'm fully conscious and pushing 'Prince Charming' away. At first, I thought the fear and anger was coming from the heart and soul of me. Angry at myself for not being aware. Anger at God for not putting a special angel on my case to keep me from flying out of golf carts! Fear of the future. My future. Would there even be a future?

My life changed in an instant. Of course, I experienced immediate pain, headaches, and vomiting… *déjà vu*. Only now I was having the worst trauma, yet, to my head, at the age of 57! And there was fear of the unknown. How bad was this?

Little did I know the extent of the damage that had been done. I would find that I could no longer read without my eyes jumping. I couldn't write more than two sentences before my handwriting became illegible. I couldn't think of words that I needed to say. When tired or stressed, which was much of the time after this, I had a hard time with speech. And I continued to suffer excruciating headaches, with loss of bodily function and massive vomiting at times of higher stress, or even seemingly at random times. Later, I came to realize how thoughts about the accident, or talking about it, could trigger major incidents.

Losing the ability to read and write, my two favorite pastimes, was emotionally painful for me. Much of my business revolves around them. Travel is also a big part of my wellness business. I have family in many places, as well, which required travel for me to be able to visit, but traveling became difficult for me. Change in pressure was another assault on my fragile brain, leaving me with massive head pain and vomiting to the point of dehydration.

Unfortunately, I got on a plane the day after the golf cart accident, to fly to Utah. My dad was not doing well, and I needed to be there. I went against the advice of a nurse who had come to buy product from me. She took one look at me and said, "I don't like the way you look," but I felt I had to go. I had to make sure Dad was ok. So, instead of resting the 48-72 hours that I now know is crucial, I took an eight-hour flight, and ended up in bed the next day with an intense headache and throwing up.

Emotionally, I was a mess. I would swing between anxiety and depression. Depression for the loss. Loss of the proper functioning of my body and brain. Loss of the ability to do some of my favorite things. My health and wellness business was suffering, because I got anxious standing in front of people and teaching when I knew my speech was affected. My memory was not the same, and I was no longer the person I had been. I went from speaking in front of sometimes hundreds of people about wellness, to becoming almost a recluse. Home was my refuge.

That is why, months later, feeling lost and alone on that dark road, I was scared, angry, and confused. I had been on the phone with one of my sisters, on my way to a cooking class with one of my business partners. My sister and I were crying together about a friend of hers who had been raped and murdered in her own home, with her two-year-old present. In my state of mind, and with a 'broken brain', negative thoughts and crying triggered headaches and stomach issues. It triggered fear. I made it to the cooking class and realized I had forgotten to stop for gas as planned.

By the time I left the class later that evening, my head was pounding, and my stomach was churning. I took a wrong turn, and in the confusion of my brain, I felt alone and vulnerable on this dark road in a construction zone. Afraid that I would run out of gas, with a cell phone that was all but dead, I expressed my fear and frustration very vocally to God.

This was one of the lowest points of my journey. I barely made it to the gas station, where all I could do at first was rush to the restroom, lean my head on the wall, and cry, hoping no-one else would come in. After some time, I was able to get some gas in my car and get home safely. But the drama and trauma had taken its toll. My body did not want to function properly. I was sick, throwing up, humiliated, and barely made it upstairs to my bedroom. I thought, *Is this my life now?*

I praise you because I am fearfully and wonderfully made; your works are wonderful, I know that full well. – Psalm 139:14.

My hobby for many years, and my business for over a decade, is in the wellness field. Research is a crucial part of my health coaching business. Thankfully, I was doing good things that I already knew to do, to calm the inflammation in my brain. I truly believe that I had 'points in my brain account' that helped me through the first weeks, but there was inevitable damage that would be much harder to navigate in the days and years to come, exacerbated by not having had immediate attention.

Little by little, as time went on, I started researching to learn everything I could about the brain and trauma. I learned to love Audible books and video masterclasses – something I had not embraced before, because I love everything about a physical book. The feel, the smell, the rustle of turning pages - reading a book, usually with a cup of tea or coffee and snacks on my porch or in bed is a whole experience for me. Now I had to learn to make adjustments.

As I was learning more about Traumatic Brain Injury (TBI), I came to realize that much of the anger and other emotions I was experiencing, was not only the feeling of fear and loss I had, but was also a result of the physical damage that had been done to the part of the brain that controls emotions. Interestingly enough, I had found myself reaching for an essential oil blend that had been researched for a year with staff and doctors at a psychiatry center, with great results. It mainly addresses forgiveness, but was also helping with other emotions.

I was using it several times daily. I had one in my car, my purse, and on my bedside table, and don't even know how I ended up with that many. Later, I looked back on that and realized that my body knew what it needed. The 'body keeps the score'. The body knows. Letting my intuition lead the way was an important aspect in my healing, and in forgiveness.

Neuroplasticity is the most exciting thing that I have learned more about in my study of the brain. In very simple terms, the brain has the ability to rewire itself.

"Nerve cells change and adjust. In some cases, the brain activity associated with a given function can be transferred to a different location, or actually change physical structure." - Costandi, Moheb. Neuroplasticity.

Although there is more activity and success in younger brains, there is still hope for those of us who are older...

Hope is what I chose, and continue to choose.

Even though I did not initially do one of the most important things after such a serious head injury – to rest for two to three days – I had some things going for me, like good nutrition, supplements, and knowledge of and access to products that support a healthy inflammatory response. However, I knew there was more that I could do, and I had a long uphill climb. Another plus in my 'healthy brain column' was the love of research and learning, because we have to be our own advocates and do the work. Hope needs a hand.

2017 was a pivotal year for me. I had a new product that had helped patients with post-military PTSD. I knew it was going to help my anxiety and depression and assist me to be able to focus more. Challenging myself to learn new things is fun for me! It is more work when dealing with the effects of brain trauma, but it is also a great path toward rewiring the brain.

One of my goals before the injury was to get my health coach certification. I decided to go for it, as this supplement was helping me beyond my expectations. I knew the course would not only be stretching and expanding my mind, and be helpful to reinforce the healthy living I believed in and needed to be doing more of, but it would also increase my influence to help others. A year later, my course was completed and I got my IIN Health Coaching certification. I got to check one of my 'bucket list' items off, too!

Earlier that year, my husband had bought me a mini golden doodle, because he knew I loved them, and he thought she would be a good 'service dog'. The day he came home with Rory, I held this tiny ball of fur in my arms and laughed and then cried. I wanted her for a companion, but I knew I didn't have it in me to care for her. After only a few days, I told him I could not do it. He took over the care, feeding, and house-training, and I simply got to love her and receive love from her. Unfortunately, her training for service dog did not happen. She has too much personality and loves people too much! But Rory has brought me joy and comfort. A girl's 'best friend', with not many expectations and no judgement! I know her companionship has been helpful in my moving forward, especially during that year.

When you get into a tight place, and everything goes against you till it seems as if you couldn't hold on a minute longer, never give up then, for that's just the place and time that the tide'll turn. – Harriet Beecher Stowe

Over the years, there have been multiple modalities that have helped me to get to the point where I am today. Not perfect, but much more present, focused, confident. I knew I had made great progress when I heard my grown daughter and son talking one day while they were sitting beside me on the couch. I heard the word "Mom", and jokingly asked, "Are you guys making fun of me?" I had just been talking about something. I don't even remember what the conversation was about. My daughter said, "No, Mom. We were saying how much better you are doing. You're almost back to yourself."

That was a pivotal point for me. Hearing those words was encouraging and motivating. One of the main things I struggled with was no longer feeling like myself, and feeling like I was a burden and a failure. It brought tears to my eyes to hear my kids say they noticed the improvement! Here was concrete evidence that the work I was putting in was making a difference, and that my brain was doing its part!

I still struggle with some of the fine motor skills. My handwriting is not perfect. When I'm tired or under stress, it is a little harder to express myself. When

I'm not following my own protocols, I am definitely more anxious. I can get weepy and depressed more easily, but I also have the tools to snap back from the mood swings, and deal with the ways that I have had to adjust in certain aspects of my life.

I know I have much to be thankful for. I survived what many don't. I have gotten through some really hard years. I've gained invaluable information about how to have a better brain that I have been able to teach others, which is important to me. My mother has Alzheimer's, also known as 'the slow death', so I try to be cognizant and always working towards better brain health. I know that brain injuries increase the chance for Alzheimer's. That is why I will continue to learn and do more to be my own best advocate. I know that what is good for the brain is also good for overall health, which is my goal.

Do I always do the things I should? No! Do I fail to do some things I should? Yes! Movement is sometimes my biggest nemesis. And movement is crucial for my health. I've learned to turn on 70s music almost daily, and just dance! I learned to line dance on YouTube, combining movement with learning new patterns, which is good for every brain. I take long walks with Rory through a forested area of our property, getting sunshine, aromatherapy from the trees and plants, and movement all at the same time, as I barefoot through our trail. I am breathing in healing and hope and breathing out gratitude and joy at what I've been blessed with.

*Let today be the day you give up who you've been for who you
can become.*
— Hal Elrod

2020 was a year none of us will forget. My biggest milestone on this journey of healing was the day I got on a plane by myself and flew to Prague for ten days of training and fun with leaders in my industry. I am an introvert. I was a middle sister who would not go anywhere by herself. And I had a 'broken brain'. How in the world was I going to get on a flight to Prague, with a long layover in Frankfurt? But in February of that year, that is exactly what I did, with the encouragement of my husband and adult kids.

Do you know what my initial thought was? Why aren't they afraid for me to do this? Don't they realize how intimidating this is? I will be on my own going through customs, and on my own for hours in another country, trying to navigate through a German airport speaking English, and get on a connecting flight and stay in a hotel by myself, prior to meeting up with the rest of the group. I will be tired and stressed. What happens if something goes wrong? What if I miss the connecting flight or the bus? I can't do this. My brain is 'broken'. Why don't they care?

And then I realized something that gave me courage. *They know I can do this! They know what an amazing experience this will be.* They had confidence in me, when I didn't have it for myself. But I did it! I even added a last-minute experience in an old district, at night, all by myself, before flying out. Now that I'm initiated in traveling to Europe alone, I'm ready to do it again. For me, this was a huge boost to my confidence, and I felt like I could do anything after that trip.

I saw a mug at my aunt's house that said, "God gave us music so we could pray without words." I know that music is magical. It is a gift. It has the power to soothe a troubled spirit and bring joy. Before everything shut down in 2020, I took guitar lessons – something that has been on my 'to-do' list for years. I plan to get more lessons so that I can join my grandkids playing around a campfire in the backyard. Someday, maybe I will put to music some of the poems I wrote while doing 'brain dumps' of my emotions during this journey of healing.

I have come through a valley of darkness, where I learned how resilient my brain is and how strong I can be, with help from friends, family, and the one who formed me. I continue to study and learn more and more about this beautiful 'broken' brain, and how to improve daily. Although I take some steps back occasionally, I'm always looking ahead to the next opportunity to do better, whether taking masterclasses, dance classes, guitar lessons, or doing more self-care – and being available to help others become stronger, too.

Thank you, Lord, for leading me in ways I never dreamed of. You brought "beauty from ashes and the oil of joy, instead of a spirit of despair". You never did forsake me.

Fly away,

You can fly,
'Cause your broken wings
Made you beautiful
To the one who knew.
And he made you new.

Out of the ashes
Like the Phoenix rise.
Your life brand new,
His Healing in your eyes.
Though you're broken,
You are beautiful.

Inspirational Insight

Some of the positive steps I took to move forward with my life were...

Even though I got very little medical help, I had already formed good health habits that took me through the first year of just basically surviving. These were: good nutrition and supplements, essential oils for inflammatory response and neurological support (especially frankincense), barefoot nature walks, and music, meditation and prayer while sitting outside on my porch with my morning coffee.

Having a hard time reading and writing, I started listening to Audible books, and writing small snippets, and then realizing I could just speak my thoughts into notes on my phone.

Mindset work, breathing techniques, learning to do habit stacking (from *Atomic Habits*) adding more modalities of movement, and learning and challenging my brain, were all healthy practices I added as I was able.

Making sure my mornings are quiet, peaceful, and meditative has been extremely important in my healing; although a good dance around the kitchen many days while coffee is brewing, or a stroll outside, can be a great precursor to a beautiful morning on the porch.

If you are going through similar challenges, I want you to know...

there is hope and there is help. You must be your own best advocate for your health. Get immediate help. And rest before you get to work fixing your 'broken brain'.

I wish I had known...

I was not alone. There are many people who have had TBI. More is being discovered all the time about our beautiful brains. Find a good neurologist, but also, be open to many different options and opportunities to improve your brain, whether you've had an injury or not. I didn't have much concern or follow up from traditional healthcare. Again, be your own best advocate.

I was Beautifully Broken.

I am now stronger, wiser, more confident, and curious. I'm ready for more adventures! Most of all, I'm extremely grateful.

Dedication

This chapter in my life is dedicated to my family, friends, and biz partners, who witnessed first-hand the change and loss of my health, my personality, my speech, and more, as a result of a traumatic brain injury. They supported me in so many ways, and trusted me to continue to be a wife, mom, grandma, friend, and entrepreneur, while navigating through the trauma, the research, the many modalities, and the healing. Thank you especially to my husband, David; my grown-up kids – John, James, & Brittany; their spouses/significant others – Tara, Blair, and Chris; and all their kiddos – my amazing grandchildren, who make me smile the most, and motivate me to do more. We're still on this journey together.

About the Author

Lois has been described as passionate, and a good listener, with 'quiet strength'. Also called bohemian, and 'so 70s', she loves music and dance, walking barefoot through the wooded areas on her property in Land O' Lakes, Florida, and creating with many different mediums.

As a child, you could find Lois in a tree, or hiding in a closet reading. These days you can join her on her porch for tea and a good book, journaling, and conversation.

As a researcher, health coach, and multipreneur, Lois likes to use her listening and empathy strengths to help others find their path to healthier living spiritually, physically, and mentally. She enjoys cooking and experimenting with good food and cuisines, and loves hosting cooking classes. Her home is always open to her family and friends, whether around the fire, or the pool. The more the merrier.

Lois loves to travel, but her favorite thing is spending time with her husband, kids, and grandkids. Last, but not least, she loves the companionship of her walking and porch partner, Rory, an adorable mini golden doodle.

Connect with Lois...

Website: theloislane.com

Email: loislaneessentials@gmail.com

IG: loismlane

FB: Lois Marie Dean-Lane

Book Projection 2022/2023 – Serenity Now: Musings & Recipes

You Don't Have to be Brave in Order to do Brave Things.

Anita Swetman

Where was I? How did I end up here?

As I stood in the huge hall, I could feel all the eyes in the room staring deep into my soul. They all knew why I was there. *But how could they know? Or was it all in my imagination?* I was 'thinking' that they knew. Then, at that very moment, all I wanted to do was turn around and run away. But I couldn't. Everyone was looking at me. I froze right where I was standing, dead in my tracks. Fear had paralysed me. I couldn't move. *It's too late now!* I cried to myself, But I had come this far, there was no turning back now.

But was it too late?

***

It was August 2003. I was getting married the following month to my soulmate, when I experienced my first wake-up call. If I had carried on with what I was doing, working in a career that wasn't what I wanted to do, I would never make it to an old age. As I felt all eyes on me, I slowly came to as I lay there on the floor. I didn't know where I was at first, and I couldn't feel anything down the side of my face.

"Just look at your eye!" my colleague said. What had just happened?

A year after my incident at work was when I first experienced a vision, a dream. It was so strong, and it was of me being the proud owner of my own beauty salon. But I didn't know anything about being a beauty therapist or running a business. I was a pharmacy technician! So, I dismissed the dream. I forgot about it, and I carried on being stressed out and tired. I carried on doing what I was doing every single day. Because I didn't know any different. I was stuck in my rut. I was *waiting* for my life to change.

It took a very long time before I realised that the only person that could change my life was me! I was very happy in my relationship, but not in my career. And considering I spent more time in my career than with my now husband, I knew I needed to change things. I just didn't know how at the time.

The dream had kept on coming back to me, night after night. It grew stronger in my mind, and I could actually see myself in this new way of life. Then my negative voice came creeping in, and I'd ask myself, "What makes you so special that you can change your life? You've chosen your career, stay safe! It's a dangerous world out there, you might fail!"

A few months later, a friend of mine lost her daughter without any warning to an undiagnosed health condition. It gave me another wake-up call. It reminded me once more how precious life is, and that life was too short to stay in a career that was making my life miserable. It was this shock that made me finally take action and pluck up the courage to take a leap of faith and look further into what my dream was trying to tell me. I was so, so scared, but I just took it one step at a time.

It was at the beginning of 2005 that I finally stood there in line with all the 17-year-olds at the local college. Yes! It had taken me another year before I actually started to research courses at college for the qualifications that I would need to start my business. I had kept on putting it off. And even when I was there with all the other students, I felt like I shouldn't be. *Me, a mature student at 35? Why am I putting myself through all this? What makes me so special that I can be a student again and learn another career at my age? I'm too old for this! Stay safe in your corporate career. Stay inside your bubble of comfort. You don't need to make yourself feel uncomfortable.*

These were the words that kept on going round and round inside my mind, trying to talk me out of doing something new and different. I froze and could feel all eyes in the room looking at me, judging me. But they weren't; it was all in my imagination. I felt though, as if something – or was it someone? – was pushing me towards the lecturer. The feeling started to grow stronger, and as I calmed the noise down in my mind, I told myself that no-one was actually judging or looking at me. It was as if I was meant to be there. Although, I was very scared! But scared of what? No harm was coming to me! So why did I feel this way?

When I was six months old, my family and I had moved to a remote part of Scotland. My dad wanted a better way of life for myself, my mum, and my elder brother. We never mixed with many people, as the village was tiny and only 30 pupils attended our local school. When my Nan passed, I was just ten years old, so we had to move quickly without warning back to the southeast of England. We left our little bubble in Scotland to move back to an area that my dad had feared for his daughter. He had loved our way of life and didn't want to go back to where he had been raised. It wasn't really a bad area, but it was very populated and busy, and he kept me wrapped up in cotton wool. My dad was so protective of me that I wasn't even allowed out of the garden gate without him! I don't regret any of this, as it has made me into the strong, ambitious woman that I am today.

When my sister and I had to start our first day at the local primary school of over a thousand pupils, we hung onto our mum for dear life! We were screaming, crying, physically and mentally scared! Can you imagine the scenario? I look back now as I write my chapter for you, and I cringe. I wish I hadn't been like that. I wish I hadn't been scared and could have done things that other children my age did normally, but I had learning difficulties at school, and there were some subjects I just couldn't grasp.

I was so frightened to put my hand up and ask for help in case I looked stupid in front of the class. When one day, I did finally manage to put up my hand, I was told to go and sit down and work it out for myself. I couldn't, so I never tried to put my hand up again! That was how I found out about my learning difficulties. I couldn't work things out for myself. I needed a lot of help and patience.

But would I have changed anything, looking back over the years? No. I wouldn't change a single thing, as I realise that this was all experience. Experience of life! We all have different experiences of life, good and bad. You choose whether to let it control you and stay that way, or you learn how to go on and lead a normal fulfilling life. But it's not easy. The long road to healing and finding what you want to do with your life will take as long as you allow it to, and there are no rule books on parenting. My dad thought he was doing what was best for me.

In November 1991, my dad left this world, when I was just 18 years of age. He was only 54, and I watched him fight for his life in front of my eyes. Nightmares and depression haunted me for years, and I was left in this world, a frightened little girl without my shadow to protect me. *How could I go on living a normal life with no-one to protect me from harm?* It did happen, but not until many, many years later.

I went through too many bereavements and tragedies to get to where I am today. But it didn't JUST happen! I had to learn how to go on and live a fulfilling life. It didn't come easy, and I made a lot of mistakes that cost me years of my life.

Procrastination. I kept putting things off! Procrastination is the killer of hopes and dreams. It's better to arrive late at your destination than not at all! But when will you be ready? Trust me, you will never be ready. You just have to dive into that ocean.

Fear of the unknown is what holds us back in life. But there is no magic crystal ball predicting our future. Our future isn't even written yet! You choose which path to take. Whether it is right or wrong, you just won't know until you try.

"But what if I choose the wrong path?" you ask. "How would I know, Anita?"

You won't know, until you take that leap of faith. If the path doesn't feel right, then you travel down another path! I certainly have travelled down a few different paths to find the right one, and with every mistake I made, I grew. With every mistake, there is a learn. You learn what isn't working right so you can make sure you don't do it again. It's with all these mistakes that I made that I am now a very confident woman, and the proud owner of my successful business. But there is always room for improvement, as I am growing further out of a 'new' comfort zone. Just never, ever give up on your dream.

"But I've chosen my career, I've studied hard for years and invested so much money, time, and energy," is the usual response. "I can't change now. It's too late. I only know this life. I haven't a clue on how to change things, I have a mortgage to pay. Mouths to feed. I'm scared!"

When you become sick and tired, of being sick and tired, you will find a way. You will receive 'wake-up calls', which is the Universe's way of prodding you to follow your heart and your dreams. Don't wait! The time is now. Don't leave it like I did. I learned the hard way. I experienced a health scare, which then prompted me to start my business after qualifying to be a beauty therapist. But it wasn't until six years later, when my lost my elder brother suddenly to an undiagnosed heart defect, that I finally took the leap of faith to leave my *safe* corporate career behind for good, and go full time in self-employment. I worked my way up whilst still in my corporate career, so I still had an income coming in. But how did I manage that when I was working full time? I studied at night school at the local college, and all the nights when I wasn't at college, I turned the TV off to study and build my portfolio for my exams. I found a way.

But how could I turn a part-time business into a full-time one, and quickly? It's no secret. I got myself out there. I pushed through my fears to create my business and doubled my income in the first month! Then I continued to do that every, single, month!

"So, how do I start, Anita?" you ask. "I don't know what I want to do!"

The best place to start is to look at what your interests are. What do you enjoy doing? Do you have any hobbies? Even if you don't have any and have lost your way in life, there is no need to stay stuck where you are. You are worthy of becoming the person you dream of becoming! You can do this! Yes. You. Can!

Visit your local library or search online. Start at A and work your way right to Z. There may be many things that may grab your interest, so look into them all. Find one, just one that lights up a fire within your soul. Once you open up your mind to the possibilities, you may even find a few that ignite your fire! I can honestly say from my heart that when you find something that you may enjoy, look into what you can do to make that interest into earning an income from it. Or maybe it could be a new hobby for you. If you don't wish to start your own business, but need something to make you feel alive every day, then you are partly on your way. Just trust the process and go out there and look at what it entails to get you to where you want to be.

Just take it one step at a time, and then the path will be shown to you. You never know, what starts out as a new hobby may even create another path as you progress down the line. It certainly did for me! And you will start to attract opportunities as they come towards you when you open up your mind and start visualising about becoming the person you dream of becoming. But *only* if you keep an open mind. Your inner radar will home in on what's required to get you to your goal.

Life and success are a journey, never a destination. Keep on growing and learn how to become a student again.

I'm scared! I kept telling myself. *I can't do this!* Every time I moved further out from my comfort zone, I experienced heart palpitations, sweating palms, and feelings of wanting to throw up. These are all normal reactions when you start to do 'different' things than what you are used to. And there were many times I wanted to give up on my dream, feeling that it wasn't worth putting myself through all this discomfort. However, I look back now and I'm so pleased that I did push through my fears. Otherwise, I wouldn't be here now inspiring YOU to never give up on your dream!

With every step that you take, you are moving forwards. For me, it was always one step forward and four steps back when I was procrastinating. I never got anywhere, and stayed stuck where I was. But as I grew further, it turned into three steps forward and one step back. Then when I published my first ever book, I was moving three steps forward and *no* steps back. As I write this chapter for you, my ideal reader, I am still, and always will, move forward in my life.

Never look back; you are not going there. Whatever you have been through in your life, you can either let it get the better of you or you can choose to win! It's not easy, and you will need to learn how to develop a mental, physical toughness to survive. But there are many self-help books that can help you on your journey, so find out what's best for you.

I thoroughly recommend *Feel the Fear and Do It Anyway* by Susan Jeffers, and *How to Stop Worrying and Start Living* by Dale Carnegie. I remember my dad had a copy of this book when I was young, and he always kept it by his bedside. It must have been there for a long time, as I know he read it frequently.

It's strange how I ended up with a copy of this same book when I was 23 years of age, but it was meant to be, and maybe it was my dad who had guided me to read it. As if he knew I needed it, too. I was a shy, introverted worrying mess when I was growing up, being kept wrapped up by an overprotective father who was frightened of me coming to any harm.

***

My heart was pounding so loudly, I felt like at that very moment it would explode from within me. I knew I didn't have long to wait, though. The categories were all flashing up online in front of my eyes. I couldn't wait. I was getting so impatient! My heart started pounding louder and louder. It must have seemed like an eternity, then finally they announced my category: Beauty Therapist of the Year. They always saved the best till last – I guess it's the same as at the Oscars, with Best Actor/Actress the biggest and best title of all!

It was at this point that I started to doubt myself. Now? Yes! My head was going into overdrive. *You won't even get bronze. You were a fool to enter these awards. You're not good enough. Whatever possessed you to think you, yes you, would win gold?* I look back now and realise these last-minute jitters were perfectly normal. But they didn't feel normal to me at the time.

I sat there in utter shock!

As tears rolled slowly down my cheeks, it was out there. It just happened. I couldn't believe what I was hearing and seeing…

'Don't let your past dictate who you are, but let it be part of who you will become.'
- *Louis Mandylor*

To be continued…

Inspirational Insight

Some of the positive steps I took to move forward with my life were...

I read so many positive motivational books and listened to YouTube podcasts to help improve my mindset and confidence. It wasn't easy, and it was a long road of self-development to become the person I dreamed of becoming by reprogramming my subconscious mind. I also developed a daily habit of learning the art of self-gratitude. Learning how to live in the moment, and by meditating daily to help keep my mind calm, clear, and relaxed.

If you are going through any similar challenges...

just be gentle on yourself. The long road of self-development takes as long as it takes. You will read so many books and listen to podcasts until you find the ones that light a fire within your soul. Only then will you start to move forward in your life.

I wish I had known all those years ago...

that the only person that could have changed my life was me! No-one else. As I re-read my own published heart-led story, I look back over the years I wasted, waiting for my life to change. Why did it take major bereavements and adversity to make me sit up and say, "Enough is enough! I'm sick and tired of being sick and tired!"

Then, most importantly, to take the inspired action to move forward towards changing myself and my future?

It's better to be late, than not at all, though. Don't wait. The time is now. Yesterday has gone; tomorrow isn't promised.

I was Beautifully Broken.

I am now free to be the person I always wanted to be.

Dedication

I dedicate my chapter to those who feel they want to move out of their comfort zone, but are feeling too scared or don't know how to make that leap of faith.

About the Author

Anita, who lives with her husband in Warwickshire, United Kingdom, is described as a kind, caring, and calm lady, who has strong positivity and determination to help other people.

She is a very proud stepmother to two amazing children, and is also a national multi-gold-award-winning beauty therapist and massage therapist to A-listers.

When Anita is not busy in treatments with her clients, hard at work with continual professional development or writing, she can often be found out walking round her lovely village or spending quality time with family and friends.

Her mission is to reach out to everyone who wants to change their direction in life but lacks the self-belief. You are worthy of becoming the person you want to be, and you can have the career you dream of, even if you don't know where to start the change.

You too have the power within yourself to change the course of your future.

Anita had her first book published in February 2022, *No Ordinary Girl*, which is available in paperback, eBook, and Kindle on Amazon. Also in paperback from all major online bookstores around the world.

Connect with Anita

anitaswetman@btinternet.com

www.anitaswetman.com

www.instagram.com/anitaswetmanauthor

www.facebook.com/anitaswetmanofficial

The First Steps Back

Laura Bentley

April 2014

The phone call!

I'll never forget the day I got that call, the one that changed my world for the next four years – well actually, forever!

There I was chatting away in the village hall to all the other mums while our children took their dance classes, just like every other week, when my sister called. I stared down at my phone thinking, *This is an odd time to call.* Let me explain. My sister has three children – a daughter who was three years old at the time, and twin boys who were just about to turn one! So, to call when they weren't all in bed for a chat was odd!

As soon as I said 'Hello' and her reply was, 'Hey, where are you?' I knew something was wrong. You know when you suddenly feel sick and your heart skips a beat, and I don't mean in a good way!

'Ok, it's Mum!'

I walked out of the hall and into the car park as my sister started explaining how Mum had been rushed to hospital after having a seizure.

I remember thinking, *Oh God, that's a bit crap!* But it got a hell of a lot worse than crap!

She went on to explain that Mum had had a scan and they had found a brain tumour.

At this point I sank – well, I might have even fallen – to the ground, and sat on the kerb, mouth wide open and in utter shock.

This is where I should explain that my Mum had previously had breast cancer, having had a mastectomy, chemo, and radiotherapy, but we had known it was likely to come back.

But in her brain?!

What was I supposed to do now? Should I go over and see her? But I needed to be 'normal' for my two young children. One was still dancing her little heart away without a care in the world, while as I sat on the kerb outside with my world shaken, turned upside down, and broken into little pieces. That may sound extreme, but that's how it felt!

'What the hell are we going to do?' I asked.

'I don't know, but we just need to wait until she sees the oncologist and doctor.'

My sister always stepped up when the shit hit the fan, and tried to keep things calm.

And that was it. I had to put my 'Mum' face back on and keep going.

That night my mum didn't even want to talk to me, which I totally understood. We messaged, and I left her to deal with the information she had just received with my stepdad. I was struggling to understand it, to work out how I was supposed to just carry on, so God only knows how she must have been feeling.

All I wanted was to go and see her, and for my mum to tell me it was all going to be ok. But I couldn't. It was her that this was happening to.

I felt stunned, angry, lost, scared, and the worst thing of all was just not knowing what this meant – like, really meant!

The next morning, I got up for my job as a behaviour support assistant, and took my children to school, just like any other day. But as I walked down the long corridor to my classroom, I was trying to hold back the tears.

It felt like I was just drifting along in this cloudy bubble, not really hearing anything around me. I didn't really want to see anyone; I didn't want to talk about it; I didn't have the answers for myself, let alone anyone else!

Why was I even here? But what else was I supposed to do: sit and wallow at home?

Don't be blinded by it.

My mum's cancer was terminal, and it was just a matter of managing it now.

Her treatment began with a craniotomy. How crazy to just pop open your brain and remove something from it!

We never heard her complain or show she was scared. The only thing she did tell me once was that she used to stand in the shower and say, 'For God's sake, what have I done? I've only ever tried to be a good person! Can you just piss off now, I'm not having it!' Imagine if you had been outside the door hearing that!

I was determined to go and see her after her operation. Why so determined? It should just be easy to go and see your mum, you might think. And yes, it should, but I hated trains. I was so nervous on them, and she was in London! I also had to make sure my husband was around and okay for me to go; that's just how it was in our marriage.

And I went. Putting my brave face on. First, to get on the train, and second, to see my mum and not burst into tears!

There she was in her bed, looking like she had just come out the boxing ring, with a huge bandage around her head. But jokes aside, she was talking normally and that was a massive bonus and relief. Whilst I was there, they came to remove the bandage. Just my bloody luck!

'What does it look like sweetie?' she asked me.

Bloody hell! Her whole head had been cut in half and stapled back up!

'Yeah, it's good, Mum, it's like a hairband! It goes from ear to ear, right across the top!' I assured her.

'Really? I thought it was only going to be a few inches!'

We had a giggle about how she could be the new Frankenstein, and discussed some of the other patients on the ward, wondering what they were in for.

While I was there, they came to do some tests to see the muscle connection, and I sat and watched as she closed her eyes and moved her arms and hands as instructed. She thought she was moving them exactly as the doctor had asked, but in fact they were in a completely different place when she opened her eyes.

She laughed, but I tried not to cry!

During the next few years, she took on any treatment she needed, never once showing us if it was getting to her.

I felt like I was always waiting for the worst.

My sister and I went to see my mum's doctor, to discuss any questions we might have. She explained it was like firefighting, they were putting out each one as it came, but there would be a point where the fire was just too great.

One of the best bits of advice she gave us was, 'Stop looking at the sun. When you look at the sun, you get blinded by it. Stop looking at death and her dying, because you're getting blinded by it!'

That made total sense. I needed to stop thinking about her dying, and live in the moment.

We were now on a memory-making mission, while also trying to keep things 'normal'. We had to stop being stuck on whether it was her last birthday or Christmas, but each time I took a photo of us all together, or her with all her grandchildren, I felt as if she knew why. And every time that broke my heart a little.

The time came when she was having treatment on an inoperable tumour. She had started to lose feeling in one side of her body, and was often falling over and couldn't get back up.

The other thing you should know about my mum is that she had always been an independent lady. Young at heart, she would run around with her grandchildren, play silly games, and be 'up with the kids' as she once put it! So, it was starting to get to her that she was having to rely more and more on her husband, and on my sister and me.

The decline in her health was rapid. She had had treatment, but within roughly two weeks she was in a wheelchair, as she couldn't walk unaided. She had lost feeling in her arm, hand, and foot.

Don't get me wrong, she and I had some giggles as I tried to push her up the hill back to her house! Kerbs are not your friend when you are pushing a wheelchair – just saying!

14th August, 2017

Another dreaded phone call from my sister. I mean, bless her, it's always her that seems to have to make the phone call! She really is a true big sister, and has always been my protector!

It was the summer holidays, sun shining, radio on, back door open.

My husband came walking down the garden from his office. He was on the phone, just staring at me. Then he walked into the house and hung up.

'You need to go,' he told me. 'That was your sister. Your mum's in an ambulance going to hospital.'

What? Wait! I was just messaging her an hour ago, and she replied! She told me she liked my new jumper and hoped the kids had a good day! She was eating a roast dinner with me yesterday!

I got my shoes and drove! I have no idea how I got to the hospital, it was about a 50-minute journey and I don't remember any of it!

When I got there, there was a queue for A&E! I must have been bobbing about like a Meerkat, looking for my chance to pounce and get in!!

There she was, with my sister and stepdad, unconscious.

That just shows how life can change so quickly!

The tumour had not responded to the treatment, we were told. In fact, it was now swollen and bleeding.

This was it. This was the fire they weren't going to be able to put out.

The hospital was just awful, and not where she needed to be. They were trying to find a bed at a hospice, but they were like gold dust.

The next day, as I walked into the ward and passed the nurses' office, I overheard them say, '…at the Hospice of St. Francis, but we have to get her there by 3pm.' Could this be it?

The Universe had answered us, and we found ourselves in the most beautiful place that we couldn't be more grateful for.

Mum suddenly seemed much more relaxed. She had her eyes open and was holding short conversations. There was a little glimmer of our mum.

We spent three long and painful weeks at the hospice, and I drove backwards and forwards on the 50-minute journey, in my own little world.

When I say painful, I don't mean we sat and wallowed every day. Far from it. My sister and I would go for walks through the grounds and woodland, sitting on a bench looking across the fields, being grateful for each other. And we were grateful for this peaceful place that had scooped us up just when we needed it most, and was allowing us our final days with our mum.

Just outside my mum's room was a pond, and I would sit for hours watching the dragonfly darting about in the sunshine. The painful parts were watching Mum slowly slipping away. When we first arrived at the hospice, we had some funny conversations as she flitted from reality to reaching for things that weren't there! But gradually she went from responding to our touch as we held her hand, to not even opening her eyes any more.

I felt guilty for leaving her at night in case she needed us, in case I wasn't there when she took her last breath. And I barely slept, as I checked my phone all night, thoughts whirling round my mind, my stomach in knots. I felt guilty for not being with my children, for not giving them a fun summer holiday. All I wanted to do was be selfish. To not have to think about anything or anyone, just my mum and my sister. The pain was getting real.

As my mum started to fade away, we all slept at the hospice – me, my sister, and our stepdad. It was like one big camp out, and my sister does not do well on little sleep! Mum would have been laughing at us.

The day my world stopped

As we sat around Mum's bed, my sister and I on one side, and our stepdad the other, I could feel the change. Everything was much quieter; her breaths were few and far between, and much more peaceful. Something in the room had changed, and I just knew this was it.

We spoke to her and told her it was ok, she was ok to go now, she didn't need to hold on any more. We said we were all so proud of how she had dealt with the cards she had been given, and we couldn't have asked for her to have been a better mum or grandparent.

I wanted her pain to end and for her to be at peace, but I didn't want her not here – of course I didn't.

When she took her final breath, tears trickled down our cheeks, my sister holding Mum's hand and squeezing mine tight. I felt like I couldn't breathe. Our journey at the hospice and with our mum had come to an end.

We all went back in and said our goodbyes individually. Mum looked so peaceful, with flowers now on her pillow from the nurses. I sat and said what I needed to say or could think of to say in that moment! But there is always more, isn't there?

I just wanted one last proper hug from her, a proper one, not the ones we had had where she couldn't move. How could I walk out of that room and leave her? This was the last time I would ever see her again. I just didn't understand what I was supposed to do.

I suddenly felt completely empty and lost.

Outside, I sat in my car, not wanting to drive away. The hospice had been our home for three weeks and the last place my mum was. I didn't want to go back to being a wife and mum; I wanted to hide.

As I opened the door to my empty house, with no-one there to catch me, I had no idea what I was supposed to do now! Curling up on my bed I broke down and sobbed until I had no tears left. I was alone, lost, angry, confused. What was this all about?

It suddenly dawned on me that one day my kids would feel this pain, this physical pain that no-one ever tells you about, like your heart has cracked.

Over the next few days, weeks, and months, a dark cloud engulfed me. I began to feel disconnected from my life. Completely broken, I felt lost and alone, even though I had people around me. The person that I wanted to talk to about how I felt, to help pick me up and tell me I would be ok, wasn't here any more.

Instead of asking how Mum was, people were now asking how I was, and I just wanted to say crap! But I gave the classic response: 'I'm fine.'

While Mum had been ill, everyone asked about her, all the time. But now she had died, it was like no-one knew what to say to me any more. No-one even said her name. So, I made it my mission to talk about her whenever I could. To share my mum's light, her humour, her love for life, my memories – which I struggled to see for a long time – with anyone I could, just to keep her light shining.

But I want you to know that if you ever find yourself in this position, feeling lost and alone, hurt and angry, you will be ok, and it won't always feel like this.

Finding my light

I needed to get myself out this funk! So I threw myself back into exercise with full force, and slowly loved it again! Well, I hated it at times, but you know... My head started feeling clearer, and I had more energy and purpose.

So I decided to become a personal trainer, like you do, and help other people get out their funk! My husband wasn't overly impressed, but I just had to do it. And I did!

I also started practising breathwork, which I found really healing, and I began to reconnect with my true self, finding my confidence again, and feeling like I could take control of my life.

My marriage then broke down, and in whirlwind we were selling our family home and I was having to start over again. Talk about kicking a girl while she's down!

My breathwork instructor told me about a training retreat in Ibiza to become an instructor. But how the hell could I just get up and fly to Ibiza? I'd never flown alone or even booked my own flight. Oh, and I don't really like flying!

Why the bloody hell not? I hear you say.

Exactly. This was my time.

The day I boarded the plane, I was a nervous wreck, shaking, crying, doubting what I had done! But I can tell you it was the best week of my life. I had to push myself out my comfort zone and allow myself to be vulnerable, learning new things, and presenting in front of a group of people. It was intense practising breathwork and meditation every day, and I cried, a lot. I was healing from the death of my mum, the breakdown of my marriage, and trying to finding my light again.

But I flew back home a different person. I promise, I did. I wasn't shaking, crying, or doubting myself. I knew I had found my light again, and I was ready to share it.

Fitness and the power of breathwork had saved me from self-destruction and were now what I needed to share with as many people as I could. I wanted to help others reconnect with their true self and feel more clarity and peace.

I arrived back to the arms of the girl I knew had helped me see and start loving my true self, and who believed in me.

I was now feeling like the real me. I had been lost for so many years, trying to fit in, doing what was right for others and not for me. It had taken Mum dying, feeling truly broken, and my marriage to end, breaking me that little bit further, to find my true self and inner light.

Now I look at old photos and don't really see myself. My sister says I've changed in front of her eyes, back to the Laura she remembers before I even got married!

I'm still on my journey, but I'm on the right one now.

My wings were once clipped, but now they have grown back full of strength, to help me fly wherever I want to go! You can grow yours, too. I believe in you.

Inspirational Insight

Some of the positive steps I took to move forward with my life were...

getting back into fitness. Any form! Walking, dancing, whatever you enjoy.

Putting myself first for a change, giving myself the time for reading, meditation, breathwork, affirmations, time with friends. Find something that raises your vibration!

If you are going through any similar challenges, I want you to know...

it won't always be like that or feel that way. You have the strength and power within to live the life you want, full of love and light.

I wish I had known...

that it was ok to give yourself time. You don't need to rush back to work or commitments. Grief comes in many ways and at all different times. It's like a wave that you just have to ride. And however you feel is ok; there is no right or wrong way to grieve and mourn.

I also wish I had known that it was ok to be me, to do me and not follow the crowd, but to be brave enough to follow my heart.

I was Beautifully Broken

I am now being true to myself, shining my light to help others, following my heart, and living in the moment.

Dedication

To my amazing mum, Angela aka Nangie, who made me the person I am, who showed me strength and taught me to follow my heart, and whose journey allowed me to find my inner light and true self. I will always keep your light shining, Mum.

To my two amazing children, Josh and Chloe, who have accepted my decisions with open hearts and who have kept me going. I truly hope I have made you proud.

My amazing sister Claire, who has always had my back, no matter what, who has held me up and got me to see sense, and is my rock.

And to Millie, for coming into my life and showing me what my heart needed, my cheerleader who gives me that little shake when I'm having a wobble of self-doubt!

I love you all.

About the Author

Laura, who lives in Hertfordshire, England, has been described as a down-to-earth, inspiring, infectiously positive, supportive, and passionate soul.

When she's not sharing her passion of breathwork, she can be found wandering through a forest, on an adventure in her camper van, or dancing around her kitchen with the old school tunes blaring! Laura is known for her ever-changing hair colour and a laugh that could fill a room.

She is proud to have found her calling and to continue her studies to become a Master Breathwork facilitator, as well as working on local community projects.

Laura is passionate about helping others on their journey towards healing and finding their inner light, whilst showing people they've got everything they need inside of them! Together, as one, we can evolve the Universe with every inhale and exhale!

Connect with Laura Bentley

Email: laurabentley@btinternet.com

Facebook and Instagram: @dragonflywellness.uk

Soul-Two-Soul Healing

Su Pinckney

Everything happens for a reason; I've always known it. Often you don't work out why until afterwards, but it will always be there. Synchronicities are everywhere!

Years ago, I was told that I would one day write a book. I was told this again at a palm reading when I was 45. By that point, I already had the title, but that book is for another day – a direct account of my spiritual journey from childhood. It isn't all love and light and fluffy bunny rabbits on a spiritual path!

So, when I got a phone call out of the blue from Cassie to ask for some Reiki (I hadn't heard from her in 14 years!), and she then asked me to write a chapter in this book, I knew it was happening for a reason. It might not be '*the*' book, but a chapter in another one could just be the start.

'Beautifully Broken', though? I didn't feel broken. Bad things had definitely happened, but I didn't feel I had held onto them or let them break me. I have worked with Reiki for many years, and each time with a client you heal a part of yourself. So how was I 'Beautifully Broken'?

In comes Andrew.

2022 started with a feeling that changes were needed. I was considering selling my therapy business that I'd had for 25 years, but I felt I needed some guidance. When asking for recommendations, a friend suggested a soul reading with a gentleman named Andrew Hobbs. As soon as I heard 'soul reading', it resonated with me that this was what I needed. I was nervous but excited at the same time.

About the first thing he said was that Karma wanted to reward me for all the good I've done for others, that it was my time to get out into the world more, and that I would be given many opportunities from the Universe to travel and meet others. He then said I wouldn't like the next bit (I thought, *Oh no, what's coming?*) but I would be classed as an 'ambassador'. My reply was, "Ooh, no!" Anyone that knows me knows that I don't like titles, being classed as a guru, or anyone being put on a pedestal. The fact that he said I wouldn't like it interested me, because it was confirmation that perhaps his guide channelling the soul reading really did know about me!

What came next was that I first needed to heal my broken heart. Something inside resonated but I didn't know what. I didn't think my heart was broken. My mind went logical: my dad passed away; on the same day, my husband and I decided our marriage was over; many years ago, I had separated from a partner whilst pregnant. These were all possible reasons, but Andrew also reminded it could be past life wounds.

Losing my dad was hard, but he had vascular dementia for over four years, so we had lost him long before. I like to think I helped him pass over, as I held my hand over his heart, telling him how proud we all were of him and that he could go peacefully. It felt so natural, and I felt very blessed that I had the chance to do it.

My husband and I had drifted away from each other, due to circumstances of life which can take a toll on any relationship. We are still friends, so all is well.

After telling Andrew all this, I still didn't feel I could pinpoint the cause of my apparent broken heart. I even questioned myself: perhaps I'd grown such a thick skin when it came to relationships? I've always just got on with life, whatever has been thrown at me. This reminded me of some EFT (Emotional Freedom Technique, or Tapping) sessions I had had with Rebecca Martin. These had brought up and released some deep issues I hadn't realised I had stored – a deep traumatic experience from childhood, and even past life issues.

Further sessions were my next sensible step on the quest to find what the cause could be. Prior to the next session, I realised myself where it could stem from, and we used the sessions to explore and release the stored trauma and emotions trapped in my body. I had supported many women over the years who had been through a similar experience. Whilst not sharing my own, I was able to draw on it to support, heal, and guide, and allowing them time to explore a different viewpoint. I had never felt triggered in those situations, but I now realised that maybe I hadn't fully faced my own pain.

So, where do I begin? Forty years ago, when I was a young 18-year-old girl. Many things have happened since, and a lot of healing, but there's always room for going deeper to heal the soul, and writing this has hopefully given me the opportunity to do that – not just for me but for those who read this. I don't just mean older women, but also young women and teenagers that have unfortunately had to go through this experience. Men also, I would imagine, carry sadness, guilt, blame, shame, and regret after years of knowing someone – whether a wife, girlfriend, or one night stand – who went through this.

There are times when this situation is judged and criticised, which I understand. (Innerstand) But, believe me when I say this, we have been our own judge and jury for many years and carried with us the pain, sometimes not even being aware. Since re-living 40 years ago, I know I have – not just mentally, but emotionally and physically as well. This is where I forgive myself and start loving me for me, even my mistakes and past hurts. They were all lessons, after all. However spiritual we are, we are still only here having a human experience, and for some reason many of us choose this traumatic one! From that time, I have learnt many things, and that is what it's about. It's another lesson in life. Some are painful, but as long as we learn from it, that is the important thing.

Many things about that time are a blur. I was on the pill, and it was a shock. We went to see the doctor at the local hospital, and he looked at me as though I was a criminal and just said he wouldn't do the termination. I look back now and think perhaps it was because we were living together; I really don't know. So, the clock was ticking, and we needed to get two signatures to be able to have the procedure. We had to pay someone in Bedford. We visited their house, and they signed and must have put us onto the clinic in Brighton to get the second signature and have the termination. Time was running out by then. I cannot remember how many weeks I was, but I know there was an urgency.

My partner couldn't afford a day off work (I now look back and can't believe how many excuses I have made over the years; money was short, so an excuse was made), so it was my mum that came by train with me to Brighton, still not knowing the outcome. We got a taxi to the clinic.

Mum left me there and began probably the saddest journey home for her. Later, she told me the taxi driver said to her, "She will be alright."

I remember being gowned up and waiting to go down to surgery. I was to be the second one to go. There were a few of us, but I only remember that from afterwards when we were back on the ward and seeing them with visitors. I had got talking to a couple of the ladies who came from the Seychelles. Apparently, it was illegal for terminations in that country, as it still is for many, I believe. I just remember one had long dark hair, and I think she had had an affair and fallen pregnant.

As I mentioned, I was the second to go down and was the last to come back to the ward. The others were saying they were worried about me, and they could all hear me screaming! All I remember was hearing a soft voice saying, "Susan, Susan," and I began kicking and screaming and sobbing. I heard a nurse say, "Ouch!" Apparently, I'd hurt her whilst I was kicking out.

On the ward at visiting time, I remember lying there watching the others with their visitors, and just going back to sleep.

Next, I had to face my journey back home. I don't recall the taxi ride, nor even the train journey. What I do remember is feeling as if I was looking down on myself, watching from above. I met my mum and Nan at a shopping centre, but how I got there is a blur; I guess a taxi. It all seems so surreal. My Nan didn't know I'd even been away, let alone what I'd been through.

Back home at our new home. I walked in and saw an azalea plant on the dining table from my boyfriend. I don't recall much else from that time, but afterwards I hated azalea plants, and every time I saw one it must've triggered the emotion of coming home to an empty house after my traumatic experience and finding just that on the table.

As I said previously, life is about lessons, and it is up to us if we want to learn from them. After all, we all have free will.

So, moving on, a few years later I moved to another location and new job. I thought it was the best option, as my relationship was one of those off and on ones, and would finally end. But, after a while, my ex got in touch, and so it all started again (I know, you don't have to raise your eyebrows!). I didn't say I learnt all the lessons! The Universe obviously thought I had a bigger lesson to learn, and after a short while, I once again fell pregnant – again whilst on the pill.

A few months before, I had been extremely poorly with aching legs and stomach problems. I'd been to the company doctor, but she couldn't find anything wrong. I was tired and lethargic but the pains in my legs were the worrying symptom at the time. Eventually, after a second internal examination (I'll spare too much detail), she pulled out a very manky looking tampon! Amidst my horror and embarrassment, she said, "You aren't the first, and you won't be the last." Due to the fatigue, it was recommended that I take Vitamin B5, which I have since found out can possibly weaken the pill, possibly causing diarrhoea.

So, there I was again: same bloke, in an on-off relationship, and pregnant again. Unfortunately, I became poorly and there was a possibility I could lose the baby. I was advised to have complete bed rest for at least five days. My dad picked me up, as I wasn't allowed to drive, and I stayed with my parents. I had a visit from the boyfriend, bringing me an energy drink

(I have never ever drunk any since!) before he headed off to the local pub. After a few days, I was back on my feet, and all was well with the baby.

I remember going round to the boyfriend's house before I headed back home, and halfway through a film I told him we were two different people and that I now had another life to look after, not just mine, and basically drove off. I don't remember everything clearly, but I vividly remember holding my tummy and saying, "It's just you and me now." And that's how it was!

I always dreaded the day I might see the ex again, and after a few years that day came. Funnily enough, it was one of the first times my daughter was at a birthday party, and I didn't need to stay. I nipped to the local shop, and there he was sitting in his car. My heart was pounding, and my head was full of thoughts and feelings, but I strangely felt strong.

I remember him asking me questions and saying, "Just tell me and it can be a chapter in your book." (Ironically, it now is a chapter!) I replied, "You are the chapter, and that book is finished!" and walked away. To this day, my daughter still hasn't met him.

Once again, moving forward, it was time for my daughter to choose her university. As you know, I don't believe in coincidences, and after visiting a few around the UK, guess where she decided she loved straight away? You guessed it – one just outside Brighton! I had always vowed I would never go back there!

At that time, I hadn't told my daughter about the termination. I'd always had in mind that if she found she was pregnant at a young age, I would let her know and support her in any decision she made. But the situation never arose, and when she did fall pregnant, she was at an age where she was able to look after a baby and be a wonderful mummy.

It did play on my mind for years that I hadn't told her, and I guess I was ashamed and disappointed in myself. The fact that she hadn't ever met her biological father was bad enough, although that didn't stop her from having a lovely childhood and growing up to be a level-headed, beautiful lady.

There have been many what I call 'spiritual synchronicities' throughout my life, and it's only in writing this chapter that I realise there were many more that I would like to share.

They say that spirit chooses a baby's name, and my daughter is called Apryl. If my first pregnancy had happened, its birthday would've been April.

A few weeks after having the termination, we got a dog and named him Buddy. He had been born on the day of the termination.

Then, of course, there is Apryl's love of Brighton.

Years ago, to get a pregnancy test, you had to go to the chemist and wait for your result there. After my first positive result, I ran out of the chemist in shock and straight into the path of a car. The driver was my boyfriend's dad!

***

Once I had decided to write the chapter for *Beautifully Broken,* my head began whirling with thoughts. The fact that I still hadn't told Apryl at that point; wondering what other people would think; wondering if it would ruin the other authors' stories. I began talking to friends that I knew wouldn't judge, and they encouraged me. Finally, I told Apryl my dark secret, after one of my EFT sessions which brought up more of what I had gone through and allowed me to clear the judgement on myself.

Apryl did what Apryl always does, and let me be. She gave me the most loving hug and allowed me to cry and talk. I even explained about never wanting to go to Brighton again and she said, "Why didn't you say?" But I couldn't, because I hadn't shared it and the time wasn't right then.

When she was young, I always called her 'Angel Apryl', even before I was interested in angels spiritually. She's like my guardian angel, and I have always said she is my soul mate because I believe we learn from our soul mates. Thinking about it now, I perhaps had my first lesson when I was an innocent 18-year-old who wouldn't say boo to a ghost. Now I connect with them graciously!

Also, from that young girl, I've grown up to find my warrior spirit, standing up passionately for what I believe in. Rights and wrongs, I don't blame anyone from this experience, as we are all on our own journey, trying to deal with things that we sometimes can't possibly imagine we would have to. No-one knows until it is thrown at you, and you are in the situation. It has made me the person I am today, and I am very blessed and grateful that Apryl and I have the relationship we do.

Throughout many years of giving Reiki to women that have gone through a termination, and many that have lost babies through miscarriage, I have learnt that the soul of the child decides if it's ready to be here on the Earth's plain. Sometimes it decides it isn't ready, for whatever reason, and often it's a lesson for the two people that conceived and are going through lessons themselves.

Interestingly, since starting to write this chapter, I've met and supported two ladies who have recently gone through a termination. And that confirmed my initial feelings were right that this needed to go out to a wider audience. After all these years, it still carries such a stigma, and perhaps that's why it's not talked about.

I've written this chapter of my life without fluffing it up, as I call it. I just wanted to tell my story as it was and is. That is my personality; what you see it what you get – no frills. Much of it is a blur because, as I said, it was 40 years ago, and perhaps it's been my protection to not remember it all. Just because I made my decision, like many women, it doesn't mean we haven't felt loss, grief, sadness, regret, and dislike of ourselves, without the added outside influences judging us. Due to this strong stigma, it can be a taboo subject and not talked about, too often 'buried under the carpet', as the saying goes.

I have decided to finally open up, hoping that more ladies/men do the same, even if it is just to me. As my nan always said, "A trouble shared is a trouble halved!"

Inspirational Insight

Some of the positive steps I have taken to move forward with my life were...

well, my Reiki practice, for sure. I knew as soon as I heard about Reiki, I felt emotional. When a friend said she had just been on an introductory talk about healing, I literally had goosebumps. Another synchronicity stepped up, because my parents were away on holiday and had left me with £350 for something useful, and it was almost that amount to learn Reiki then, which was about 28 years ago. I didn't tell my dad for years how much it cost, but to me – even to this day – it was money well spent. I finally started doing something I needed to learn that resonated, and I began a wonderful journey of self-discovery and healing, for me and for the hundreds of people that I have met over the years. Strangely enough, it was Christmas money this year that I used for my Soul Reading and my EFT sessions. Once again, the money was there at the perfect time!

If you are going through any similar challenges...

I want you to know that you really aren't on your own, although it may feel like that. There are people you can talk to, and I am hoping to set up a support group that will be a private space for all of us who have experienced this – either yourself, or perhaps a loved one or friend who has confided in you. Again, it will trigger our own emotions, and I will be writing a book solely on this.

I would like to acknowledge the souls that didn't walk the Earth plane, or the ones that decided to do it at a later date that they chose, so that they too can experience life as a human being, whichever journey they chose. The ones that don't, I feel, have finally learnt all lessons here and don't need to return.

If anyone wishes to share their experience, anonymously or otherwise, you can email me at su.pinckney@gmail.com. It will hopefully be the start of your healing process of forgiving yourself, and perhaps moving on in life. Writing it down has certainly been another way for me to heal. I am also available to do distance or hands-on Reiki, so please contact me on the above email, or I recommend that you research Reiki practitioners in your local area and find someone you resonate with for in-person sessions. I also recommend EFT. I had my sessions with Rebecca Martin, who can be contacted at relaxandbe@outlook.com. This can be done in person or on Zoom.

I wish I had known...

more people I could confide in over the years and 'innerstand' about soul contracts we all choose to make before coming to the Earth plain.

I was Beautifully Broken.

But am now feeling more at peace with myself, mainly because I always felt there was something I needed to tell my daughter. I am an open book, so that made me feel uncomfortable. I also wanted to tell her because she often said she thought she had been here before.

Dedication

Thank you to my mum and dad for bringing me into this lifetime, so I could live the life I was born to and find my warrior spirit. My daughter Apryl, for being my soul mate and giving me the opportunity to be a nutty nanny to Seth and Lillia. My husband Michael, for being my grounding stone and twin flame. My Nan's wise words, hence writing this chapter. And finally, my ancestors, Dr Usui, St Germain, soul tribe, and Galactic friends, for guiding me over the years.

About the Author

A young girl known as a smiler, who loved being creative, I'd save the worms on the path – and still do. Watching ghost/alien films perhaps planted the seed for my interests in spirituality/connection to spirit, and with ETs. I fight for what I believe in, and I care passionately about wildlife and nature. Consciously connecting, trusting my higher self through Reiki and meditation, many times I was told that I can't save the world. But I want to make this earth a better place for us and future generations.

Twenty-nine years ago, I started as a Reiki practitioner teaching all levels. I'm now recording guided meditations for YouTube, which I feel is a continuation of my helping people through life – something I've always been known for doing.

A bit about me from others' perspectives:

"Beautiful smile, radiating positive energy, always ready to share her natural gifts."

"You are firstly safe. Comforting, reassuring, funny, and never changing, you were these when I met you years ago. You will still be this and more in years to come, you are one beautiful soul. I'm glad I found you that day, you have improved me and therefore my life."

"You have talent when talking, put a positive spin on things. You make someone feel better about themselves or situations; I don't know how you do it. Your way with words has much meaning, can change the mindset of what someone thought was bad into something beautiful. You are an inspiration to many."

I am now enjoying life at my pace with family and friends, continuing on my spiritual journey into my 60s, and grateful for all who share my life. Many people say how spiritual I am, but at the end of the day, I try do my best. I am me.

Connect with Su

Website: www.withcomplements.co.uk

Insta: wellbeing at With Complements

YouTube: Wellbeing for awakened souls

https://youtube.com/channel/
UCZW5p3jwcDrsefdtkuy4M6w

Don't Give Up

Dawn Chivers

A t the age of 16, I joined the Armed Forces. As I left, my mum gave me a poem card, which I still have. This has guided me through life, at times of difficulty. Although at times I think I did put it in the background, instead of following its guidance.

Don't Quit

When things go wrong, as they sometimes will;

When the road you're trudging seems all uphill;

When the funds are low and the debts are high;

And you want to smile, but you have to sigh;

When all is pressing you down a bit,

Rest if you must, but don't you quit.

Success is failure turned inside out;

The silver tint in the clouds of doubt;

And you never can tell how close you are;

It might be near when it seems far.

So stick to the fight when you're hardest hit.

It's when things seem worst that you must not quit.

John Greenleaf Whittier – 1807-1892

So, where do you start writing about how you have come to live with Fibromyalgia and Chronic Regional Pain Syndrome (CRPS). There is always a beginning, but at the moment there is not an end, as my experiences and development are constantly moving to better places and situations. Don't quit.

Back Injury – the diagnosis of Fibromyalgia & Chronic Regional Pain Syndrome (CRPS)

Who would have thought that with just one move, your life could change? That is what happened. I had an accident at work, over ten years ago now, moving a patient. I injured my back, and life started to take a turn for the worst. I could hardly move that night, and the pain was so intense that all I could do was cry. Finding it difficult to work, off I went to see my lovely GP. She said my sacroiliac joint and my back were in spasm, so off I went with diazepam to relax and ease the spasms.

I returned to work, but my lack of sleep was causing havoc. I was not resting, as the pain was intensifying at night. So, I was given amitriptyline, which helped me to sleep but it also made me very snappy and irritable. I felt angry all the time, so that was stopped. Trazodone was to replace it, and this worked much better. At work, I was still struggling to complete the most basic tasks of my role. So, I was given codeine, which did not mask any of the pain, then onto tramadol. Wow, this was just too much. I did not know what I was doing and nearly walked in front of a bus. So, it was back to the GP for another medication review.

As my condition was worsening and I still struggled to do my work, I eventually went off sick, and was referred to a local Rheumatologist, due to my back going into intense spasms, causing immobility and pain. After appointments with him, he diagnosed Fibromyalgia and CRPS. I was put onto anti-inflammatories, morphine, sleeping aids, and more pain relief. At this point, I was having meetings with my manager, HR, and society representative, and it was decided that I could no longer work clinically, and I was to be redeployed into an administration role. So, that was the end of my career and my MSc, which I was near to finishing.

Feeling the loss of a career was one of the hardest things I was contending with. At the time, I did not realise I was grieving, and it has taken me years to try to accept what had happened. The reaction from my family, friends, and colleagues, was incredibly supportive, but the ones I thought would empathise with me were the ones who turned their backs.

My mobility was slowly getting worse, and I was unbalanced and falling. It was time to admit defeat and get walking sticks to help with my stability. I splashed out at a local disability shop and bought sticks that did not make my wrists hurt (rheumatoid arthritis handles), and were a bit less boring than the metal or black ones available at most places. They were a blessing, as now I could walk easier with less pressure on my hands.

I also had to apply for a Blue Badge, which would help me out so much. I was accepted after a medical, and it was such a relief being able to park near to the entrance at work and when out shopping. It made life a little more bearable.

So, it was all change in our household, and I was having to rely more on my husband and family for support and to do simple tasks. I had been referred to a Pain Course, where we got physiotherapy, hydrotherapy, counselling, and lessons on how to manage pain.

It took me a long time to understand about pacing myself. As soon as I thought I felt a good change, I would do more and, yes, I would then go back downhill. I had to learn how to try to do things but not to the extent where I was wiped out for days afterwards. I was so infuriated with my body at this point. Why was it doing this to me? As this situation slowly got to me, I have to admit I did turn to food, because I could not drink alcohol due to all the medications that I was on. As a result, I gradually went from a size 10/12 to an 18. It was such a tough time, that I just could not see a way out.

We unfortunately lost my mother-in-law, so life was changing even more. She had been there to support me during the diagnosis and had helped me come to terms with the changes.

Relocation

A few months later, we relocated. My husband would be working away from home Monday to Friday, and I was on the lookout for jobs. Changing GPs was another issue. After falling down the unfamiliar stairs, I could barely move. So I called the new GP, who insisted that I go down to the surgery, I had to book a taxi, as I knew I was in no fit state to drive.

The drive was excruciating, as the road bumps were horrendous for someone who is in so much pain. On attending, the doctor said I had badly bruised my back, but as I was obese, it was not surprising. I knew he was partially right, but my head went straight into the sand.

Having to go to the Jobcentre to claim unemployment benefit was another strange experience, and they asked if I could do a cleaning job temporarily until I could find more appropriate work. I had an education which they looked at in total confusion, questioning whether I really did have my BSc and Pg Dip because I had mobility issues. All of the jobs they offered were physical roles, but this stopped once I managed to see the Disability Advisor.

The fact was that people attended with a view to getting a job, but unfortunately week after week, I had not been successful. I lost count of the number of jobs for which I applied. At this point, I just concentrated on my crafting to make things bearable. I finally found a locum data entry job, mostly working one or two days a week, a 40-minute drive away. Over the years since my accident, I had turned to various crafts (quilting, sewing, crochet, and jewellery making) to distract me from the pain. Friends had liked what I'd made, and I was attracting more interest in what I did.

Seeing an advert for a Businesswomen's Course, I decided to see what I could learn to set up my own business. The course gave me more confidence in both myself and my creations, and halfway through the course I contacted the Tax Office and created my business. The start was ok, but what I was finding difficult was to get my goods into either shops or craft fairs. They could be fussy about who they would have, and it was quite difficult to be accepted at certain fairs.

Along with the craft insurance I needed, I had put quite a lot into my business, so I started to try to do more craft fairs, but this just caused extra pain. Trying to get everything to the place, setting up, and then sitting for hours, made my back and legs hurt even more. I did enjoy selling my crafts, explaining techniques used, and seeing the delight on the buyer's face that the item was usually unique – especially my jewellery. And people really did like my creations. After craft fairs, putting everything back into the car was the worst. I would often get home and either wait for someone to help me, or just leave things in the car. I still was not earning enough to be independent.

So I continued looking for jobs and eventually I found one. Finally, I could start feeling useful and become part of a workforce again.

A New Job & Medication

After a year of searching, I finally got a job. Working again, I felt like part of a team, but my mobility was still an issue. I would be working four days a week, and it was a different set-up to the ways I had previously worked. But I began to settle into my job, as well as life in a different area.

I had been referred to the pain clinic locally, and when I received my first appointment, I ventured out wondering what they would change. Immediately the consultant said I could not continue on the low-dose morphine I had been given and that I needed another medication called Lyrica, which would help with the nerve pain. He explained that it might take weeks to work, but it was better than continuing down the route of heavy medication, which could be harmful eventually. Within a month, the pain was becoming more bearable, and the severe pins and needles from my waist down were diminishing. I was still dependent on using at least one of my sticks, but there was a definite improvement. After a year of working in my new role, I had an impromptu meeting with a Weight-loss Consultant, who told me about a new group being set up. I decided to take the plunge and see whether my GP was right, that all my pain was due to my weight.

I did not agree entirely with him. Yes, it was affecting my mobility, but I could not imagine that every single spasm, sharp pain, pins and needles, were just due to my weight.

Losing the Sticks (Stabilizers)

I had spent six years on walking sticks, helping me to get about, albeit slowly. I hated the fact that I was in my thirties and yet I had to depend on two pieces of metal to get around and behave like others. Within five months of starting my new diet, I reached a healthy weight and had only 7lbs to lose to get to my target. Slowly my mobility had also improved; the pain was still there, but it was easier to move around.

Friends of ours had been posted to Kathmandu, Nepal, and they had invited us over for a visit for two weeks. We were so pleased, because we had previously been to Northern India, and always wanted to go to Nepal, to see such an amazing country. We admired the Nepalese people, especially the Gurkhas – most people who have served in the Armed Forces have the utmost respect for them. At the same time, other things were happening on the work front. There was an opportunity for me to work more clinically, so I applied and luckily got the confirmation of my change in role later in the year, just before leaving for our holiday.

This was a dream come true, so off we went for our visit. And this is where things changed quite dramatically. The flights and the travelling really took a toll on me. The pain was really bad, and I ended up having to use a wheelchair at one of the airports. We arrived early on a Sunday morning, so our friends said to have a rest before going out for Sunday lunch. We enjoyed our meal out, then it was back to rest for the evening and off to bed early. I was so tired that night, wondering whether I would be able to sleep, but I slept amazingly that night. Was it the high altitude? I wasn't sure.

On our first morning, I woke up feeling strange. I had not got much pain, and I was a little scared. What was going on? I felt as if I was numb in my back and legs; the incessant pain was missing. It was such a surreal feeling. I really did not know what was going on in my body, but I decided not to argue with it and we started slow, but I did not need my sticks and was able to walk without aids. It was amazing.

The whole trip was amazing – to see our friends again, to spend time with their friends was great, and to visit such amazing places. We felt truly blessed. Our visit was a year before the earthquake that hit this area quite badly.

On our return to the UK, I was still a little nervous, but my mobility was still getting better. I was able to get rid of my Blue Badge and my sticks. Within two months of being home, I hit my target weight and sustained this for a few years. I had stumbles over the years with my Fibro, CRPS, and shingles, but life was not as hard as it had been previously.

Recurrent Shingles

Over the past 25 years, I have suffered from recurrent shingles, which is so painful and fatiguing, leaving me in tears at night. Where the blisters appear makes it difficult to sit or lie down. Trying to get into a comfortable position is ridiculous with this condition. You are given high-dose anti-virals that you have to take five times a day for seven days, but they make you feel nauseous and often upset your stomach. Trying to rest is important, but at the same time you have to try to continue working, which can be difficult. If I work through a bout, then I do not do anything else that day; it just draws energy out of you so much. And although the blisters normally dry up within two weeks, the after-effects can continue for much longer.

After suffering seven bouts in one year, I began to research more about the condition, looking at research articles and a book by an immunologist. It was suggested that a Mediterranean diet would help to bolster the immune system rather than a low-fat diet, which I was following, so quite quickly I changed my diet. I was also put onto a daily, low dose of anti-virals to help prevent breakouts.

Brachial Neuritis

A few years ago, I suffered from Brachial Neuritis and was unable to use my right arm. It was another hurdle, yet again. Friends and family encouraged me to just concentrate on what I could do, so that was reading, and going out for walks on most days. Luckily, the weather was mostly in my favour.

As I got a small amount of use back in my arm, I had read about mental well-being and the power of nature bringing you back to a sense of being. So, I started to take photos of the nature and scenes around me. Although at that point I could still hardly bear anything touching my arm, I went out and bought a one-shoulder daysack, and stuck to my vest tops or very loose cotton shirts. Every time I got dressed, I had to think about what I was about to put on. It was quite depressing, as each texture could cause me so much pain.

Although I was getting out, I felt only a minor change in my mood. I was still unable to do the things I loved – baking, cooking, crochet, and sewing. My life was passing me by, as things had become monotonous. Eventually, a sharp pain went down my arm, changing the sensitivity of the skin and the intensity of the pain.

I could finally start to use my arm, and had to relearn how to hold a knife for chopping, although my husband still had to cut any meat as I didn't have the power to do this. I found a massage therapist who was willing to see if she could help with muscle tone and to reduce the pain and inflammation.

I was concerned that I was about to lose yet another job/career due to my body not functioning properly, so I pushed for physiotherapy and did all of the exercises that were suggested. The physio was impressed that I had walked through this, as my mental health was much better than she expected.

I was slowly starting to come off the diazepam, which had been prescribed for the spasms in my arm. These tablets left me feeling out of time, I did not always realise what I was doing, and I felt that life had lost its lustre. But with the help of essential oils that I had been introduced to, I could finally say goodbye to the loss of control feeling. I still have days where I know I have done too much, but to have most of my mobility back in my arm is a blessing.

Changing your lifestyle is hard, and it took me quite a while to actually achieve this. After procrastinating about my weight and mobility, I started to take back control of my life. My goal was now to manage my situation, instead of it controlling me. To regain strength in my legs and back, I started to swim and use a steam room.

After the visit to see friends in Kathmandu, where I had experienced so many changes to both my pain levels and mobility, I visited my GP who thought the changes were due to the high altitude.

I continued to enjoy walks with my husband and friends, and years later we booked a walking holiday in Southern Italy. I went nervously, not sure how I would cope, but I managed to do most of the walks, resting at night, but achieving so much more than expected. I had proved that I could do more, just as long as I planned and paced myself. My next achievement was to see how far I could get up Mount Snowdon. I managed to get just before the halfway house, and I was ecstatic. Walking had become such an important part of my recovery and maintenance of my conditions.

After having a massage during my brachial neuritis, I was introduced to the benefits of essential oils. I was put into contact with a lady who teaches about the uses of oils and also well-being, and she changed the way I look at life and how I deal with it. If my body starts to react to a trigger, then I reach for my oils, yoga, or meditation. I am a walking diffuser most days and love the way I can adapt. I can also focus on my mind, body, and soul, to what heals me and changes my reactions. This has had such a significant impact on my life.

Over the last few years, I have started to write. It started in April 2020, when I was listening to my usual Radio 2 Sunday morning programme. The vicar delivering that day's "Pause for Thought" said that we should write our prayers down on a Sunday and then reflect on what we had written. So I started. They were short at the beginning, but this soon changed, and I was not only writing prayers but reflections of what was going on in the world and in my heart. I have now published a collection of these, and hopefully by the time this book comes to fruition, I will have completed another.

I never thought that I would be capable of writing or that I would find so much peace from it. I share my writings on a weekly basis with people who enjoy and find peace from them. I feel honoured to be able to write and cannot wait to see where this goes. Life is too short to waste it. Do what you love, love others, and be kind always.

Needing to prove to yourself that you are worthy can be quite intimidating. Through tough times it can be hard to really believe in yourself, and often people just hide and let the world pass them by. I was not going to let this happen to me, and like the poem that my mum gave me suggests, I may well rest, but I will not quit.

Inspirational Insight

Some of the positive steps I took to move forward with my life were...

stopping comparing myself to others, putting myself first with self-care, using my oils, yoga, walking, and meditation, to help concentrate on my health and well-being. Changing my diet has also helped with various symptoms.

If you are going through any similar challenges, I want you to know that...

you are not the only one. You can make positive changes to your life. By taking a look at what you need and what you do not, identifying simple changes to your lifestyle can help with both your mental and physical health.

I wish I had known that...

I could change my outlook on life, and that there were many others going through the same challenges and struggles. Reaching out to others supports both yourself and them.

I was Beautifully Broken.

I am now living my life, by adapting my lifestyle to become the person I aspire to be.

Dedication

I dedicate this chapter to my mum and husband, who have consistently supported me through both happy and difficult times, and their love and care has encouraged me to strive in life. Also, thanks go to my friends who have given me so much inspiration and support over the years, helping me to become a better version of myself. I cannot in words to express just how much love I have for all those who have been my rocks in the water, steadying me when the waters ran wild.

About the Author

Dawn Chivers, who lives with her husband in Leicestershire, has been described by friends as lovely, caring, compassionate, creative, amazing, incredible, inspirational, and a chatterbox. When she's not working, she can be found in the craft room, creating quilts, jewellery, bags, and crochet. Dawn also enjoys walking with her husband, taking in the nature that surrounds us all, and which inspires her to write reflections about the experiences she comes across. She has also learnt the values of yoga and essential oils in her life, to help with the stresses of the day. On a Sunday morning, she will be found listening to the radio whilst writing her prayers, sending them to friends around the country, and maybe even further afield.

Dawn gained peace and connection during the pandemic lockdown by writing prayers, reflections, and taking photographs, then sharing these with family and friends, who encouraged her to publish them as a record of what was happening through that time. She published *Pandemic Prayers and Reflections from the Heart* in 2021, and will soon be publishing a second collection, with plans to continue writing. She's proud to have served in HM Armed Forces, and attends local Veterans' Breakfasts, where support can be found for everyone. She's proud of never giving up and with a mission to share love and grace with others through her writing and with each person she meets.

Connect with Dawn...

Email: reflectionsbydchivers@outlook.com

Facebook & Instagram @reflectionsbydawnchivers

Little Girl Lost… (at 51)

Sheena Doyle

"I'm so sorry but there's nothing more that can be done."

Was he really saying that to me? The paramedic was looking at me with concern and care as he came out of Mum's house to speak to us. But how could this be?

I had only seen her at lunchtime, before taking my kids into Edinburgh to meet friends who were visiting from Yorkshire. I'd waved and said, "See you later." The kids were off school for one of the many random local bank holidays that exist across Scotland, and they were excited to meet our friends.

We had eaten with them in Edinburgh, and then got back home in time to sit down and watch the Queen's Diamond Jubilee concert. I would call Mum later and see if she was enjoying it. I had been chatting with Mum at lunchtime about the concert, and she was really looking forward to it, especially Shirley

Bassey. She loved Shirley Bassey. The four of us sat down to watch it together.

My phone buzzed, and I lifted it up to read the message. It was my friend, a neighbour of Mum's. *"There's an ambulance at your mum's. I think you should come."*

My stomach churned and my mind went into overdrive, but I didn't want to panic and upset everyone. *What had happened? Why hadn't her carer called me?* I jumped into my car and rushed to her house, leaving hubby and the kids to follow.

I pulled into Mum's driveway and her carer was sitting on the step, visibly upset, smoking a cigarette, and trying to calm herself down. "I'm sorry, I'm sorry," she kept saying, but she wasn't really making any sense. The paramedics were inside the house. I tried to go in but was told to wait outside, so I went into my friend's house, feeling anxious and scared. My friend tried to keep me distracted and we chatted about anything and everything, not wanting to acknowledge what might be happening.

My husband and children arrived, and we sat down at my friend's, not knowing what to do, not knowing what to say, too scared to think about what might be happening two doors down the road. My mind was a jumble of thoughts: *Why did I go into Edinburgh? Why hadn't I popped in on the way back? Why hadn't I phoned her when I was driving home? How the hell could I have been eating pizza when she needed me most? Please let Mum be ok. I'm not ready to lose her, even if I am 51.*

The kettle was boiled and tea was made, as we waited anxiously for news from the paramedics. Mum always made tea in time of crisis. It's a Yorkshire thing; a cuppa fixes everything. My husband went out to check, and I met him outside with the paramedic. I knew by the look on their faces it was not good news.

"I'm so sorry, but there's nothing more that can be done," he told us.

Mum was gone, and there was nothing I could do. My husband held me tight, and I just felt empty and lost. As he led me into Mum's house and up the stairs, my legs were like lead weights, my brain was numb, and I felt like a child again, so scared and so vulnerable. I was so afraid what I was about to see, but knew I had to face it. Mum should be in the kitchen making a cuppa, as she always did when I arrived. A cup of tea will fix anything, and usually cake, but not this time.

The paramedic guided me into Mum's bedroom, and as I crouched down beside my beautiful mum, I began to feel this must be all a bad dream. It just couldn't be happening to me. I stroked her face, kissed her, and told her I loved her. The paramedics were kind and said all the right things. It was her heart, and she wouldn't have known much about it, they told me.

But I hadn't been there for her last moments. We were always there for each other; I had let her down. *Was she in pain? Was she calling for me?* I would never know the answers. If only I could have been there; if only I had called in to see her on the way back from Edinburgh; if only I could have had five more minutes with her and know she hadn't suffered. If only I could have said goodbye.

How was I going to tell my children? I had no time to prepare. They were waiting for news, but not the news I was going to give them. I went back to my friend's house and gently told them that Nana had gone. Our friends put a warm blanket of love and care around us whilst we tried to take in what was happening.

The police had been called, which is normal practice when someone dies suddenly at home. I didn't know that, though, and it just felt like an unnecessary intrusion at such a raw moment. As we sat downstairs in Mum's living room, the policemen tried to make conversation and take my mind off the reality and pain. One of the officers knew a close friend of ours who was also in the police, which was a distraction and took me down a different road for a few seconds. Then the wave of pain and emptiness took over again.

It still seemed surreal. I would hear her voice in a moment asking if I'd seen Shirley Bassey, asking how our trip to Edinburgh had been, asking if we wanted a cuppa. But no, I would never hear those words again, never feel her tight hugs again, and never hear that distinctive laugh. I was now alone with my childhood memories.

I went to bed at night, holding on tightly to these memories, feeling lost. I couldn't sleep. I didn't want to sleep, knowing the first few seconds awake would be fine until reality hit like a punch in the stomach. I just wished I could have five more minutes with Mum.

Suddenly I was overwhelmed with grief, not just for Mum, but Dad, too. I realised that I had never really grieved for Dad, as I had been so focussed on looking after Mum. The grief hit me so hard that I could hardly breathe. My husband was there for me, but I had no siblings, no cousins, no-one to share childhood memories. Three had become one. I was an orphan. I felt broken.

As you may have gathered, this was sadly not the first time I had felt the pain of losing a parent. Let me take you back to June 1st, 2008. Yes, the same random, local Scottish bank holiday weekend. Dad had been ill in bed for a number of weeks. The prognosis was not good, and we knew his illness was terminal, but I was still in denial and wanted to ignore what was clearly staring me in the face.

Saturday, the 31st May, was a strange day. Dad was clearly struggling, but Mum was adamant he was ok and didn't need the doctor to be called. She was in denial, and just didn't want to face the inevitable. Nor did I, so I went along with it. My husband was trying to bring a sense of reality to the situation and very gently suggesting that perhaps letting the doctor have a little check on Dad would be a good idea. He could clearly see what was happening.

Eventually, I persuaded Mum, and said I would make the call. But then I faced the frustration of our NHS out-of-hours service. All the time I was telling myself that the people on the phone were only doing their job, but this was my dad who needed help. My amazing dad, who would help anyone, so why couldn't they speed things up to help him in his time of need? Eventually a doctor arrived around midnight, checked over Dad, and gave him something for the pain. Mum stayed downstairs, just wanting to pretend everything was ok, so suddenly I was the adult. Yes, I know I was an adult, but I mean in the sense of dealing with my parents; I had to take over, take the lead; and support Mum.

The lights were dim in the house, there was a strange calmness in the room, and Dad was sleeping. *Maybe it was going to be ok*, I thought to myself, knowing deep inside that it wasn't. There was almost a mistiness in the room, and the doctor's face appeared through the haze as he took me aside in the hallway.

"I am really sorry, but your dad is unlikely to make it through the night. You need to prepare your mum," he said.

Was he talking to someone else? This wasn't my dad he was talking about. My dad was invincible and was going to get better.

Two days earlier, in between long periods of sleep, Dad had quietly told me, "Look after your mum for me, please."

"Of course," I'd replied, not really taking in the significance of his words.

Dad had always been there for me and Mum. Our little unit of three, always there for each other.

Suddenly, that three-strong unit that was my security was about to lose its strongest part. The doctor gave Dad something extra for the pain and left, telling me to call NHS24 if things changed. *What did 'things changed' mean? For the good? For the bad?* I knew the answer really.

I sat with Dad as he fell into a deeper and deeper sleep. He was slowly leaving us. My lovely dad, who was 40 when I was born, but never ever appeared like an older dad. My dad who was running around a tennis court with me in his fifties; my dad who showed me the importance of showing respect and kindness to others; my dad who was the bravest man I knew when he lost most of his sight at 62, just after he retired. He never complained, never felt sorry for himself, but now, at 85, he could fight no more. And as he drifted away, I knew I had to fulfil his wish and look after Mum for him.

"Please send someone, please," I pleaded with the NHS24 call handler.

"I need to go through some questions," was the reply.

The same triage list as the first call. No call history, just as if I had called to say I had stubbed my toe or cut my finger. I lost it! It's not like me, but I shouted down the phone, "Don't you understand? My dad is dying here, and I need the doctor to come back now!" Yet I knew inside that the doctor could do nothing any more.

Before the doctor arrived again, I held my dad's hand. He was drifting away, and as he took his last breath, there was an air of calm in the room, a kind of peace that was almost saying he was ok, he was ready. I wasn't ready to let him go, but who is ever ready to let a loved one go?

Experiencing death at close quarters for the first time brings so many emotions, and I was so close to falling apart. Mum was in pieces, and it was my turn to step up and be strong. *How was I going to do this?* I would get the strength from Dad's love, and the need to make him proud and carry out his wishes. His words sounded in my ears again: "Look after your mum for me."

I could do this; I could do this for Dad, and for all the times he wiped away my tears and fixed things for me. *Come on, Sheen*, I heard him say, *you can do this.*

The doctor arrived and confirmed the heart-breaking truth, and then started another process, one that was to be the hardest of my life to date. Mum was so lost. Her life partner of over 50 years was gone, and the pain was etched on her face. I knew then that my grief would have to be parked somehow, as Mum needed me more than ever. I had to do this for Dad. My mind started to wander. *Who would I have my football chats with? Who would ask me if I was really ok? Who would I watch 'Question of Sport' with?*

I had to stop these thoughts, otherwise I would not be able to cope with what lay ahead, and I was determined that I mustn't let Dad down. The one thing I knew I still had to face was telling my children that Grandad had gone, and just how do you do that? Well, you do get the strength from somewhere, but I will never forget their 11- and 9-year-old faces looking at me and the sound of their deep sobs. But that was a sign of the strength of the love they'd shared, and the beauty of all the memories they carry with them every day. That's what I would do, too, in time, but not yet as I had to be there for Mum.

Life without them...

She's an only child, she'll be spoilt.

She's an only child, she'll get everything she wants.

She's an only child, she'll never cope with life's challenges.

These are all comments regularly and flippantly said by others who have no understanding of the intensity of being an only child. It began to feel as a child that I was in some ways disadvantaged by this and there was something odd about it, yet I was happy, so why did people think like that? I prefer to say I was enriched with love, but not money and possessions. I was enriched by two people whose whole focus was loving me and being there for me.

The challenge comes when they are gone, but the love they provided helps you deal with the challenge. It's now ten years since Mum died, and there have been some poignant moments during that time which have helped to put back together that broken 51-year-old. Losing Mum opened the doors for me to start to grieve for Dad, too. It was a double hit, and very hard for me.

I had remarried the year after Dad died, but it was a tough day for my mum. I took strength from the chats Dad and I had had about the wedding, and knew he would want it to be a happy day. My son gave me away. He was just ten years old. My daughter was my bridesmaid; she was 12 years old. The pride I felt looking at them and knowing how proud Dad would be brought an extra dynamic to the day. When my ten-year-old son stood up and made a speech, there wasn't a dry eye in the house. Happy tears, though; tears of love and pride for the part my dad played in my children's upbringing. It felt like he was there, a part of the day, his positive and loving influence shining through.

The hard times don't tend to be anniversaries for me, although that Scottish bank holiday in June does hold a lot of sadness. I'm not someone who puts this all over Facebook every year. I just quietly remember all the good times. Memories are so important and are always there to help you through when times get tough. I talk to my friend of 58 years, who I can share some of the childhood memories with, and we laugh and cry together. This is more important as I grow older, as you value the importance of memories and how important it is to continue to make memories for your own loved ones.

The difficult times for me have been the moments when I wish my parents were there to see my children's achievements. Football games, musical theatre events, graduations, first jobs, first homes – just generally having great kids that grow into great adults.

Mum and Dad played a part in not only shaping me but them, too, and they live on through all of us. My children are 26 and 23 now, and I am incredibly proud of them. I am facing life without them as they fly the nest and find their own way in life. But I will always be there for them, as my parents were there for me, and they have the added bonus of having each other. My parents helped and had a positive influence on me bringing up my family, and maybe this will be the next chapter for me. Being an only child had its challenges, but the joy of it is the memories that live on and keep you going in those difficult moments. My parents live on through me and my children, so how can I ever really be alone?

Inspirational Insight

Some of the positive steps I took to move forward with my life were...

around keeping my parents alive through memories and conversations. I took strength from the wonderful memories and talked about them to people who also cared for my parents and were important in their lives. I talk about the small but powerful things that trigger the memories. Mum's Yorkshire puddings were the best, and the smell takes me right back to the wonderful Sunday lunches that she orchestrated with such precision and love. This triggers chats around the table about Mum and Dad, and makes me feel like we are still including them as we eat together. We chat about

Dad's amazing stories, his magic penny trick that any child that was ever in his company would be amazed by! Their love for me is alive in all these memories. I do this all the time, and I have regular conversations in my head. *What would they do? What would they say? How would they feel?*

If you are going through any similar challenges, I want you to know...

that you will learn to appreciate the uniqueness of being an only child. You will heal, you will recognise and be grateful for the unique family unit of three that has shaped you into the human being you are today. You will be stronger than you know, and the joy of the memories and the strength of their love will help you through.

I wish I had known...

that the future would bring with it a gratitude for such loving and caring parents, whose devotion did not make me any more flawed than the next person. They gave me a pride in who I am and where I came from. I wish I had known to ignore all the gossip about only children being lonely, missing out on things, lacking social skills, and being unable to stand on their own two feet. Here I am with a trusted and loving family, close friends, and a job I love. I have taken lots of opportunities in life, and also dealt with some major challenges with a strength I didn't believe I had in me. Oh, and I can hold a conversation with anyone!

I was Beautifully Broken.

I am now beautifully enriched with memories of the past and filled with hope for the future. Grateful for the unconditional love that has kept me grounded in life. So thankful for my parents' presence and support in bringing up my own children. Their values and kindness shine through in my son and daughter – an example to us all.

Dedication

To my amazing Mum and Dad, who showed such unconditional love and were always there for me. I miss you every day, but your love shines inside me, keeps me strong, and has helped me learn how to cope without you.

To my amazing husband, Peter, I love you. Thank you for your love, care, and understanding. As another 'only child', you just get it.

To my two amazing children, Laura and David, I love you to the moon and back. I am so proud of the adults you have become. You were shining lights in your Nana and Grandad's lives and help to keep them alive through all the wonderful memories.

About the Author

Sheena, who lives in Perthshire, Scotland, has been described as warm, kind, down to earth, and caring, with a sense of humour that is rooted in her Yorkshire upbringing. When she is not supporting businesses to create a great culture through human-centred leadership, she can be found spending precious time with family and friends, playing golf, and supporting her beloved football team, Leeds United. Sheena's 30 years in Human Resources – or Employee Experience, as she prefers to call it – has brought her to a point where she believes the only way to build a sustainable business is through heart-led leadership. She says she is trying in her own small way to put the human back into human resources. Sheena promotes the provision of a great employee experience, putting people before profit. Life is an experience, and Sheena believes a positive employee experience is integral to a great life experience. Making it easy for people to be their authentic selves at work should be a priority.

Connect with Sheena

Sheena@reallyusefulhr.com

Website: www.reallyusefulhr.com

You're Stronger
Than You Think

Steph Croker

The ambulance sat outside of the house. Were the neighbour's curtains twitching? Oh yes, I'm sure they were. They never missed a thing! Inside stood my mum, me, and my dad… A while earlier, I had received a phone call from my mum. "Steph, you need to get round here, your dad isn't good."

"What do you mean 'not good', Mum?" I was sure I could hear Dad in the background shouting.

"Please just come round. You'll soon see what I mean."

Thankfully we only lived around the corner, so I rushed around to the house, leaving my three children at home with their dad. "I'm sure I won't be long," were my famous last words.

Once I was there, I saw that Dad needed help, and not help that I or any other family member could give. Dad needed medical help, and quick. It was an upsetting time, but I said, "I'm ringing for a doctor." To be honest, I think Mum was pleased I said this, and I clearly had no idea what was going through Dad's head at that moment.

"Doctor, Dad clearly isn't well," I explained. "He needs help that we can't give him, please help him." It didn't take long for the doctor to arrive.

After what seemed a lifetime, and me more or less insisting that the doctor made the arrangements for admission to a secure unit at the hospital, Dad was sectioned for his own safety. I felt awful. I had basically got Dad sent away from his own home and his family.

The ambulance arrived and I went out to greet the paramedics. I could hear Dad calling out for me, and my heart was breaking. *How could the man who was always so strong and supportive towards me end up like this?* But there he stood in the doorway, a shadow of his former self. The paramedics were so gentle and kind, giving reassurance to us all.

"Steph, where are you?" called Dad.

"I'm here. It will be alright, Dad, I promise," I assured him, tears streaming down my face.

Then the ambulance doors slammed, and Dad was being taken away from all of us… As heart-breaking as it was, we also knew it was the start of his recovery.

That evening will stay in my memory forever. Mum felt useless as to what to do, and I felt that I had let Dad down. The reality is, I guess, that I probably saved him from himself, as this wasn't the first cry for help.

I felt like I wanted the ground to open up and swallow me… this was like history repeating itself. I didn't sleep much that night, or the next few nights.

The next morning, in a haze, I got the children organised for the day and then started making calls to the hospital to find out visiting times. When I went to pick Dad's clothes up and bits and pieces that he would need, Mum refused to go to visit him. She didn't think he would want to see her. I had enough to deal with and didn't feel I had the energy to challenge her, so I collected his belongings and headed up to the hospital for the first visit. Have you ever set off to go anywhere and arrived at your destination without knowing how you got there? Yes, that was me! My head was pounding and my heart thumping to the point I felt it was going to explode through my chest.

I parked the car and summoned up the courage to head to the ward. The door was locked. How frightening is it to think that patients were behind a locked door, obviously for their safety and security? I rang the bell and a nurse greeted me and let me in. I was so scared, and my mind was all over the place.

"Your dad is in the lounge at the end of the corridor," said the nurse.

I started the long walk toward the lounge. Other patients were sitting in their rooms, some with visitors, some alone, others were wandering around looking lost. I asked myself what I had done. It was so sad –

not only that my dad was struggling, but all these other patients, too. The question on the end of my tongue was, what makes someone end up like this?

"Hello, Dad," I said, with shivers running down my spine. Dad sat there looking quite lost and very alone; the sparkle had gone from his eyes.

He looked pleased to see me, which was a relief, but he looked an absolutely broken man. Inside my head, I was crying, but I had to be strong.

"I need my dressing gown, Steph," were his words.

"Yes, Dad, I've bought it and some clothes and your shaving things. Hopefully you will feel better soon and come home again."

The rest of the visit was a blur to me, as I'm sure it was to Dad as well. All I remember was thinking to myself that this was the man who wiped my tears when I cried as a little girl – and also as a young woman, at times – and now it was Dad who needed his tears wiping.

I walked back down that long corridor in tears. How did it come to this? Well, I have a good idea, but that is when the story becomes more intense and very sad.

When I was about eight years old, my mum was struggling with her mental health to the point that she was diagnosed with clinical depression. Sounds awful, doesn't it? It is, and it certainly was for my poor mum.

My dad had helped and supported mum on both her good days and her bad days.

A bad day could include Dad having to wash Mum's clothes up to four or five times. Mum wouldn't move away from the twin tub washing machine, as she was obsessed with ensuring dad washed the clothes to her standard. She would constantly wash her hands, over and over again, until they were red raw, and keep checking that doors were locked; this could mean checking a door at least 20 times. I'm sure there were a lot more issues, but these were the things I witnessed her doing on a regular basis, and it was a lot to take as an eight-year-old child.

Me and my younger brother spent time in the creche at the Mayfair day centre where Mum went for her mental health treatment. As children, we liked being there, as it was fun, but it was certainly not normal. This is just a brief example of Mum's illness and she certainly struggled with it, but maybe after Dad had been supporting her, he couldn't cope any more, and it all got too much for him.

Mum, thankfully, got better, but it was a slow process. One of my memories was of us of a family going out for a car ride on Mother's Day. We went and looked around a church, and there was a bunch of daffodils for each mum in the church, so I got mine one. She was so pleased with it, and I remember her smiling. Yes, Mum was coming back to us. Happy days.

So, Mum recovered, although does anyone fully recover from clinical depression? Now, some 15 years later, my other parent was suffering from mental health problems. You are probably thinking exactly what was going through my head: *How on earth do you end up with not one but both parents struggling with the same horrendous illness? More so, is it hereditary?* Scary question, that one!

Dad was in the Addington ward for a few months, although it probably felt like years to all of us. I clearly remember the first day release he had. Sounds like a prison, doesn't it? I'm sure a lot of time the patients felt it was, although I think the prison they were in was inside their own heads. That day, I took Dad to a fast-food restaurant, as it wasn't too far from the hospital. I wasn't sure how he would feel being out for the first time, and I had been advised that he might find it difficult after being in the safety of the ward.

I felt like I was sitting next to a stranger that day, and so many emotions were rolling around in my head. I'm surprised I didn't choke on a chip, I was so upset. I could tell there was a long way to go with his recovery, but I told myself this was a start. I had seen this before, and with a lot of love, strength, and support, we would get there.

Each day was pretty busy, juggling work, family life, visiting Dad, and of course Mum. Thankfully, she had a good friend who lived next door, so she always had someone nearby to talk to for support. Over time, Dad arrived home, and things got back to some type of normality. But some things are never the same again, are they?

You may wonder whether I felt resentment and anger towards my parents because of the situation I found myself in, but my answer would be "ABSOLUTELY NOT!" My parents had always done the best for me and my brother, with amazing Christmases and lovely holidays. Obviously, we didn't get everything we always wanted, but who does?

My dad had been there to take me to A&E on several occasions, when I broke my wrist twice, and then when I cut my leg on barbed wire. It was a running joke that Mum hated the sight of blood, so he was the person who took me to hospital each time. I mean, seriously, do you know anyone who accompanies someone to donate blood, then actually needs a cup of tea and biscuit because they felt faint at the sight of blood? Yep, that was Mum. She never lived that one down! We had a great childhood, with just a few blips on the way.

Looking back now, I wonder how I coped, but 'what doesn't kill you makes you stronger', as they say. And that's very true. Anyone who knows me sees me always happy and cheerful, but believe me, sometimes that has been a mask to protect me from my emotions getting the better of me. Not many people get to know what is inside my head. In my opinion, for what it's worth, everyone has their own worries and problems, so why burden them with mine? Although the irony is, I am always listening and supporting other people.

'If life gives you lemons, make lemonade.' I love this saying, and I've drunk plenty of lemonade! This just about sums up my attitude towards what I have experienced growing up. Let's face it, we all have choices when we hit an obstacle in our lives: which path shall we choose? I can assure you, that with strength and guidance, you can achieve anything. Even the word 'impossible' broken up says, 'I'm possible'! Just food for thought there, don't you think?

On reflection, that period of time when my life was challenging and very emotional, it is surprising how I managed with everything. But it's amazing how much you can cope with when you have no other choice. I think I spent a lot of time on autopilot, as there was so much to do. But I tell you something that I have learnt, and that is that we never know how our lives are going to pan out, and it's all about life experiences that in turn make us the person we become as an adult. Never underestimate yourself. We are made of strong stuff; we just have to be aware of how to channel our energy into the correct pathway.

I know that I have inherited my strength from my dad. That man has always supported me. Even when I became pregnant at the age of 16, he just said, "You need love and support." And that is exactly what I have always received from him. His strength has kept him going, and at the young age of 87, he is still determined to be as independent as he can be – and he is.

And as for me, the girl who was once a very quiet and shy child (no-one who knows me now believes that) has grown into a very positive and cheerful woman (most of the time). I admit I am outspoken quite often, but in my opinion that is an asset as I don't suffer fools gladly, as the saying goes. I've told my story, and I can assure you this isn't even half of it, but I felt it was time to share this to raise awareness of the support and comfort people suffering from mental health issues need, and also to reassure families that there is a light at the end of the tunnel. However, you might just need a microscope to see it at first! Never give up. You are stronger than you think.

Inspirational Insight

Some of the positive steps I took to move forward in my life were...

that I ploughed my time into my family, having two more children, moving house, and eventually becoming very interested in spirituality. I learnt a lot from my experiences, and can certainly now see how I have grown since my childhood and early adulthood. I meditate each day and have trained to become a crystal therapist and do energy work. Life is all about balance, being aligned to create the best version of ourselves, and in turn this has an impact on the people we choose to spend our time with.

If you are going through similar challenges...

whether it be yourself or a loved one, I want you to know it does get better. Embrace each day as a learning day. There is so much to learn from every situation we are subjected to, whether by choice or accidentally. Remember, where there is darkness, the light will eventually shine through. A prime example of this is night and day.

I wish I had known...

more regarding mental health and how to notice signs, but hindsight is a wonderful thing. And to be honest, I was quite young at the time. I'm hoping that sharing my story will raise more awareness of how so many people suffer quite often in silence until it becomes so hard for them that they do something irreversible to themselves. There is nothing to be ashamed of. To speak out and get help encourages others to get the help they also deserve. You are not alone; together we are stronger.

My motto is: Smile at everyone; it is free, but it might make someone's day. Let's face it, none of us know what others are going through. Always be kind.

I was Beautifully Broken.

I am now fabulously fixed.

Dedication

I dedicate this chapter to my dad. Always by my side through all of life's ups and downs, even when he was struggling himself.

Thank you, Dad x

I couldn't write this without also dedicating this to my grandad who I lost 52 years ago. Although I was only six years old when he died, the impact this man had in my life is immense.

Forever in my heart, always near me x

About the Author

Steph lives in Northamptonshire, her five children and seven grandchildren living nearby. She embraces her life to the full, enjoying spending quality time with family and friends, going to gigs, theatre, and lunch dates.

She is described by her friends as a very caring, empathetic, honest, loyal, determined, and strong woman, with the biggest heart. A great listener, she always has time for others. Her bubbly personality certainly brightens up everyone's day.

Steph has always enjoyed reading books and kept getting a nudge to start writing one herself. This chapter will be in the impending book.

Steph is passionate about raising awareness of people struggling with their mental health problems, and the support that is needed for them. Along with a friend, she recently created a group 'Alternative Minds' to raise money for the charity Mind, and organised different workshops where people can come and get support, holistic treatments, or just a cup of tea and a chat.

Her mission is to get out there and show people they are not alone and that there is always hope.

Connect with Steph

crokersteph@yahoo.co.uk

Confused. Isolated. Disorientated.

Laura Hudson

The tip of my toe touches the ice-cold bath – or is it hot? The seconds flicker and the water is, in fact, scalding; the whistling of electricity radiates from every corner of the room, screeching, high-pitched, and piercing; the words you are voicing at me are simply unrecognisable noises, a cacophony, rustling, echoing, perplexing; the inner core of me is erupting, shattering my mask, and screaming from within.

On Wednesday, 8th September, 2021, at precisely 12:30pm, after 26 years of suffering, of not knowing, not fitting 'in', hopelessly struggling to keep my head above water, feeling like I am on a never-ending emotional rollercoaster, having intense meltdowns, being 'socially awkward', feeling rejected and scared, constantly feeling anxious, desperately trying to adhere to 'social norms', binge eating, blaming myself for things that have been completely out of my control, not understanding why each person sees a different 'me' (a manifestation of social masking that has been perfected somewhat over the years), feeling broken but certainly not beautiful – I finally received my truth. A diagnosis of Autism.

It is a diagnosis that I should have received when I was a child, but it was missed by education and health professionals who failed to identify the 'red flags' at each opportunity where they presented over the years. So instead, I received the misdiagnoses of Generalised Anxiety & Depression (GAD), Prenatal Depression, Postnatal Depression, and suggestions of Postpartum Psychosis. My mental health problems do not ever go away; they are not episodic, and do not present as text-book.

At just 17, I was groomed by a 64-year-old male. I was taken advantage of by men – pressured into sexual relations because I didn't know how to say no, and even when I did, my voice wasn't strong enough – that I felt I needed to please, to meet other people's needs before my own... to *fit in*. Professionals created another 'lost girl', adding to the THOUSANDS of late diagnosed and lost girls that exist out there, many with mirroring life stories like my own.

Diagnosis has, for me, been life changing. I briefly grieved for my old self, or at least for the person that existed pre-diagnosis. My grief took place during the period of self-identification to diagnosis. I had already accepted I was Autistic by the time I was formally diagnosed in September. Others around me did not process the news so favourably, and it was harder for some than for others. The diagnosis turned out to be difficult for some to accept, or even to understand. But I felt like this was now my chance to speak up, with confidence, and with pride, because I finally felt so strongly and enthusiastic about myself. I no longer feared myself. I have been recognised, diagnosed, and most of all, validated. I found something that, for years, I never realised I was searching for, and I finally *know* myself.

Fear and dread quickly rose in respect to those closest, the ones who have never actually met *me*, only my mask(s). Those who have always controlled and held my puppet strings, those I would have predicted sniggered, "Do you actually think you're Autistic? But why?" If I told them why, then I would have to drop my mask to show them…

The only way I can tell them why is by writing. Or is this essentially just another mask? Autistic masking is a survival strategy often used by girls and women with Autism, but masking has also contributed to my confusion about who I am. Today I know who I am, but I am not yet able to remove the mask(s).

When I look back over the challenges I have faced throughout my life, I quickly realise that lots of these existed due to me not growing up in an 'Autism-ready' world, and that many could have been managed much better with appropriate support. Prior to recognising and learning the many signs of Autism, my family and I had never had the answers to why I was always 'rude' as a child (I would repeatedly call, "Mum, Mum, Mum" whilst my mum would be speaking to others, and even now I struggle to identify when exactly is my time to speak); or why I was still doll-obsessed at 14, even thinking that if I terminated my pregnancy with my first daughter (I was 15 at the time), I could replace the 'would-be' baby with a reborn doll instead and still get the pram I so desperately wanted; or whenever we had 'fun' (fun being subjective, of course) days out, these would end up spoilt by Autistic meltdowns (consisting of inappropriate behaviour or phrases, lack of impulse control, lashing out, refusal to walk, or tantrums). 'Meltdowns' are something which still feel very real, though now these cause arguments with the ones I'm closest to, lashing out in terms of pushing those closest to me away, and a dangerous and 'self-destruct mode'. This is where I have to battle within myself not to complete suicide or to not self-harm.

My restricted diet and refusal to eat anything but pancakes were actually a sign of Autism, not me just being a 'fussy eater'. I am no stranger when it comes to food, but I have a list of 'safe foods' and I will not stray too far from this. Unfortunately, it does not contain the healthiest of food choices, and at times I feel the need to binge eat, fearing that there will be nothing left that I *can* eat in terms of taste and texture. It is all sensory! Some of my family snigger when I mention the issues I have with food, because they judge me solely by my weight, yet few witness me secretly bingeing.

The supermarket makes me anxious. I don't know what to buy, I feel overwhelmed by the choice, and I panic. I don't know what to make when I've bought these things, so I buy the same items, in bulk, often leaving with four 3-kilogram bags of pasta, six 5-kilogram bags of grated cheese, ten loaves of bread, and ten packs of yoghurts. Though he does not judge, my husband finds it challenging to understand, but equally he will eat anything that is put in front of him.

When the meltdowns occurred as a child, there were many contributing factors, namely, sensory overload (sound and touch), social anxiety, and the additional pressure of ensuring I enjoyed the day out as planned. Only a matter of weeks later, I would express to my mum how much fun I had had, and she of course would feel frustrated and confused because the days did not feel pleasurable at the time. I should say here that my own mum was also late diagnosed Autistic two months earlier than me, at the age of 45. She could not understand me any more than she was able to understand herself at the time, and she too was a young mum, giving birth to me at the age of 19.

My mum and I add to the thousands of so called 'Lost Girls' who were missed and later diagnosed. I am sure you can imagine just how many 'professionals' descended on us when I became pregnant! But they ALL missed it. Why? Because, to date, not enough professionals have been taught to be Autism Aware, so they do not know the signs and miss them even when they are obvious.

I decided (yes, planned, case in point) to become pregnant at 15, and became a mum at 16 because I so desperately wanted to fit in. I saw an identity in 'motherhood' that I believed would help me to do so. What I did not realise at the time was that there was no identity that would help me to feel I fitted in, because I still did not truly know who I *was*.

Autistic people never feel like they fit in, despite grasping at neurotypical ideals that we feel will help us to do so. And the reason for that is because we live in a neurotypical world that does not allow us to – your world. It does not accommodate Autistic people; it alienates us further. We adapt, we mask, but that is exhausting and causes an influx of mental health problems, and then we get further lost in a mental health system that does not sufficiently train its professionals to be Autism Aware. We get missed…

A year prior to my teenage pregnancy, my mum had reached out to the very same professionals because of the challenging behaviour I was displaying, and which she was managing at home. But she was made to feel like her parenting had failed. A year later, when I was pregnant, those very same professionals realised it was not simply the case and there were challenges within the child, though Autistic traits were still not recognised. I ask one thing of you today: open your minds, hold back your judgement, and think beyond what you see in front of you. Because that pregnant young lady you see may have more going on than you could even begin knowing.

My diagnosis has relieved so much pressure and guilt that I have been carrying around for years. I desperately want to say sorry to everyone I have met over the last 26 years, but how can I relieve the guilt by apologising for just being ME? This is a typical Autistic trait; we apologise for everything we are. Inevitably, every person who has crossed paths with me will 'know' a different me, a different mask. I cannot help this. It's like being at the opticians, when the optician changes the lenses, but only marginally. "One or two?" you are asked. And that is the only way I can describe my masking. Key parts of me do not change – my values, my beliefs – but the exterior, the social part of me, will appear different from one person to the next.

Please do not dismiss Autism as just 'traits' or 'anxiety' or a person's 'social awkwardness'. Let those Au-some individuals own it! Please do not undermine the challenges we as Autistics face daily, including the challenges faced by the people holding us up. Please do not tell me that I am 'high functioning', as this just dismisses and ignores my struggles and vulnerabilities. I low function too often to be categorised as either. I am both.

Please do not tell me that 'everyone is on the spectrum'. If this were the case, then 'it' [Autism] would not exist. Please just accept that when someone tells you they are Autistic, they are identified, and they are proud. Do not underestimate a single one of their abilities…

Many will agree that becoming a parent is one of the greatest blessings in life. It is equally one of the greatest learning curves that those 'blessed' will ever come to appreciate. That said, no-one prepares you, not even close, and especially not at 15 years old. Furthermore, no-one prepares you for parenting and raising children with special needs when you have (un-diagnosed) special needs yourself! Autistic parents raising Autistic children. Yes, life is hard.

As the parent of four children, three of whom are suspected Autistic, we have over the last 18 months reached out to a plethora of 'support' services. And so, the cycle continues in a cruel and tormented kind of déjà *vu*. Not one of them has been willing, ready, or able to offer support, or to refer my children to the correct professional team. Not because they do not 'believe' it to be necessary, and not because we are 'fine', but because it is simply someone else's job and not theirs. How many countless families are also suffering due to sheer negligence from so-called 'support services', I ask myself?

Our family has fallen through every gap the system has to offer – and not one generation, but three! My maternal grandmother is, without doubt, undiagnosed Autistic. She has lived the life of a 'Lost Girl', who remains unfound at the age of 71. We even had the support of a private (self-funded) pre-screening assessment, which recommends a full Autism assessment to be completed for two of our children, 100% of the children we had initially raised concerns about in respect of their behaviour and emotional wellbeing. So, at what point do you give in and accept that you are alone, and the support is not forthcoming?

I am in a constant battle of overwhelm, anxiety, frustration, and perplexity. If my child had a physical disability, as opposed to a neurodevelopmental disorder, I wonder if more support would be offered. If my child were paralysed and required a wheelchair, would one be denied? Would the 'gate-keepers' still 'gate-keep' then? In fact, one of my children now *does* require the use of a wheelchair in order to keep her safe when out, yet still her school refuse to support the use of this. By refusal, I mean they actually refuse to allow the use of this to meet her needs.

My GP laughed, physically laughed, whilst questioning the school's request for a medical report detailing why this is an appropriate way to 'keep her safe'. The GP's response was, "We would not refer if we did not deem it necessary. We would not prescribe a wheelchair if it were not required for support." Wheelchair Services also added their support.

But the school defend their position with, "We need more evidence, because… and I'm not saying you are… but some parents lie about these things."

We [I] have endless volumes of evidence, each child assigned a lever arch file detailing each concern, appointment, report, diagnosis. Why are parents of children with neurological disabilities being forced to jump through hoops and beg for non-existent support? I am at constant breaking point, and there is literally nowhere and no-one to turn to. I am being forced into no other option but to consider home tutoring my child, due to the trauma which failing to provide sufficient support in school is creating.

But… and here is the big one… they woefully underestimate the tenacity of a broken woman, a mother who is defying the odds already, and a mother who will fight for her children like she fought for herself. A lioness protecting her cub(s).

When you are expecting a baby, no-one hands you a textbook or survival guide on how to parent a child with a disability, or in our case, a child(ren) who is being denied access to the appropriate services and support that they so desperately need. As a 'Lost Girl' for 26 years, I simply cannot sit back and watch my children being lost by the same system I was, my mum was, and her mum, too. I cannot sit back and watch history repeat itself time and again. I never want to see my children experiencing the level of pain which I have endured. The pain which I am reminded of every day because my multiple traumatic memories are so vivid.

Motherhood brings a darkness, a taboo. No-one speaks about the days you cry the whole way home, the days you feel like giving up, because that ball of fire in you that keeps you fighting for their every need is fizzling out, where you feel like you don't ever want to wake up, or the days when you could just walk out on your family, because life's just too hard and you question if someone else could do your job better than you do.

No-one utterly understands the reality you are living. People try to relate, but they often fall short through well-meaning comments, parents of 'neurotypical' children offering 'neurotypical' parenting advice.

A special needs parent does not need to be told what they can do to get their child to sleep through the night, or how to 'successfully' try a new meal, or how not to meltdown (the child or the parent!). We do not need advice that centres on a 'normal' family and child which meets the norms of society; we are not those things.

We want our children to be confident, proud, and accepted for who they are. And a diagnosis is key to this. It is the building blocks of their identity that will form resilience, self-esteem, and confidence. We want our children to have their needs recognised. They need someone to listen, not to be dismissed or undermined; their struggles and hardships to be validated and supported. In its purest form, their lifeline is to be heard and understood without judgement.

My children are beautiful, and they are loved more than they could ever know. Our world revolves around being special needs parents, and because of this, the fight is real. We are living this daily, and our 'hard' does not stop when our child is past the 'terrible twos', or when they start school, or when our children reach adolescence, or become an adult. Our life will be hard, the fight will be forever, and the support from friends, family, and an accepting and inclusive world, is vital.

The professionals that society holds up on pedestals, the pillars of the community, these professionals need to believe in parents, they need to recognise the signs, and they need to disregard the ideology that parent-blaming is the only answer. Their support, their belief in them that their innocent child who sees the sparkle in the tiniest detail that no-one else sees, is what keeps a special needs parent going. We accept our hard. We cannot change it, and we would not want to change our children, but we would do anything to change the world they are living in.

As I have aged and matured in my understanding and self-awareness (or does that contradict the Autism in me?), I have learnt to spot the signs and triggers from the off. I can openly say that holidays, Christmas, and planned days out, are big triggers for me, including meeting up with extended family (that is, those who do not reside in my home). I find the overwhelming sensory environment real, sound and chaos, and again, the pressure to 'enjoy myself', just too much. I can feel the meltdown building inside me. From a small spark right in my core, it grows, and I feel a numbing sensation radiating from just below my chest, down to my thighs, passing through my legs, to my toes, and right the way up into my brain. I feel out of control, angry, frustrated, and unable to rationalise or think clearly, then begin to reject the ones I love, until reaching utter 'self-destruct'.

By this point, there is nothing to pull me back. I feel impulsive and a great desire to act upon these feelings. I feel isolated and alone in my suicidal thoughts, and I begin the battle against the 'thing' within me, not to act upon these. I am left feeling exhausted, both emotionally and physically, and alone in the sense that others around do not understand, despite me not being entirely certain that I actually want their compassion or support. I end by feeling exhausted, physically, and mentally.

I am now hyper-alert to recognising these signs and triggers, and defuse (or as best possible) these same struggles which my children also experience, though this often leaves me, as a parent, on eggshells, overwhelmed, and isolated from the confines of our four walls at home. For fear of judgement and public displays of meltdowns, we often choose to remain at home.

When I reflect on the 'challenges' I have faced, I am immediately plunged deep into my mind; it is as if I am virtually transported through my life, but with a now different lens of Autism self-awareness. However significant or insignificant certain features may be, I am flicking through each specific memory, like a group of trailers for a movie, but on high speed. I can stop at each specific memory, knowing exactly where it is stored away in the world's largest library – chronological order, all bunched together, but all so separate, in a disordered but perfect formation, the details which seem unnoticeable to others, and yet are as vivid to me as they were the first time I lived them. An example of this is I can recall being in my baby bath seat (I would assume anywhere up to the age of 12 month) and I can hear the sound of the plastic balls. It is not a sound I have ever heard since, and it is almost as if I can taste the sound, too, whilst they spin and slide against the plastic bar of the seat. The intensity of this memory is real, and as I write this, I am drawn back, the sensation is real. I am taken back by such recollection.

So many girls and women are still lost and need help to be found. YOU could even be one of them. I can tell you wholeheartedly that once you receive a diagnosis and truly find yourself, your entire life seems to fall seamlessly into place. The trauma and suffering you have endured tirelessly heals, like the craters of the earth closing and sealing, flawlessly and with intention. When you learn about Autism, beyond the societal stereotypes, you begin to spot it in others you meet, gravitating towards them with interest, curiosity, and purpose – to *find* them. As you reflect upon the past, identifying the significant people you have met over your lifetime, the pieces fall into place, those connections and relationships given definition by the diagnosis. Those within whom I have seen the signs often do not have a diagnosis, and the numbers, I believe, are so much higher than society acknowledges. So many are lost, and so many are female.

In the last six months, our family has received three positive Autism diagnoses. Given the condition is highly genetic (with research suggesting this being around 90% (source: Living Autism), the statistical likelihood of my children's traits and behaviours being Autism-related is highly probable. My fight continues, but I am resilient, I am brave, and I am forever ready to advocate, to be the loudest voice for my children. Most importantly, I now know who I am, and I know my purpose.

Inspirational Insight

Some of the positive steps I took to move forward with my life were...

to raise Autism awareness in other women who are still lost and need help to be found. YOU could even be one of them. And I can tell you that once you receive diagnosis and learn about autism, you can see it in others you meet and have known in the past. I now have what I can only describe as a radar for Autistic people! Those within whom I've seen the signs do not have a diagnosis, and the numbers are, in my opinion, underestimated, and most of them are female.

If you are going through similar challenges, I want you to know, that I write this wholeheartedly in support of every 'Lost Girl'; to give her a voice, to empower her to find her truth, and to let her own her Ausomeness! My deepest desire is to raise awareness for every misdiagnosed, undiagnosed, or late diagnosed Autistic woman.

I do not know how to respond to the "you don't look Autistic" or "everyone's on the spectrum" comments, or the stereotypical comparisons which often relate to boys with autism, not girls. I'm not a mathematician, I don't line everything up in formation, I'm not non-verbal, and I am not the male stereotype of autism! I am creative, I am uncomfortable in social situations, I like facts (they're concrete and just that!), and I desperately try to break social expectations of what a 'young mum with four children' looks like.

I was Beautifully Broken.

I am now a girl who was once lost in the system of a 'boys only' club. Nevertheless, with resilience (and copious amounts of determination!), I wake up each and every morning, I take my children to school, I go to work, and I embrace new opportunities – all despite often feeling like I'm trapped relentlessly in Groundhog Day. I have four beautiful children, I am blessed with a husband who takes an unbelievable amount of sh*t and keeps me afloat(!) whilst sometimes drowning himself, I am the Rose to his Jack. I am a wife, I am a mum, I am 26 years old, I am a Business Support Officer working in mental health, but first and foremost, I am AUTISTIC. I am ME!

Remember, when you have met one person with Autism, you have met ONE person with Autism!

Dedication

This chapter is dedicated to my husband, who supports me through every hurdle, is able to say "No" when I need to hear it the most, who 'bear-hugs' me out of my meltdowns, and who stands by every decision I make. I also lovingly dedicate my chapter to my children – Evie, Isabella, Violet, and Sebastian – whom I promise I will never allow to become broken, and who will always remain beautiful… And lastly, to every single 'lost' person who is seeking to be found.

About the Author

My life has only just started. My life started on the 8th September, 2021, when I was diagnosed Autistic, because prior to that I was broken. I felt broken. I didn't belong, I never fitted in, and I've spent my whole life subconsciously searching for 'me'. I hear electricity echoing off the walls, bright lights are physically excruciating. Noise, lights, overpowering smells, busy places, I'm unable to decompress – it feels deadly and harrowing. I've often felt like a fraud, I don't 'look' disabled. I mask incredibly well. I am what the lesser aware would, and have, described as 'High Functioning'. There is no 'high' or 'low', 'mild' or 'severe' Autism; I simply have a brain that experiences the world in a different way. I've found myself relentlessly fighting with every ounce of myself to partake in 'normal'. Frantically masking myself to be verbal with all my energy, when I desperately don't want to engage in conversation, when I need not to speak.

I've experienced times where I couldn't physically speak. I've moved my mouth and the words wouldn't come out. Ever experienced sleep paralysis and tried to shout but you can't? All of this heightens my distress, yet I cannot express my needs. I've needed someone to understand and someone to help, but until the 8th September, 2021, I had no legitimacy. I felt isolated and humiliated. I've lived for 26 years without acknowledgement or support of my needs.

What I now know is that I was never broken. I was beautiful, always. At present, my children remain 'lost', but I now have the strength, the wisdom, and the tenacity to change that for my own, because they are beautiful, too. We are beautifully different, but never less. I aim to be the change that I would like to see in society, and the way that it supports Autistic people, my people.

Connect with Laura Hudson

Facebook: Just Another Mask

Email: Laura@justanothermask.co.uk

Phone: 07572696759

Metamorphosise

Donna Smith

4th January, 2022

As I sit here with tears streaming down my face, I release the pain of my past. I let go.

I release myself and others to live the life which we deserve.

I have just delivered and completed a webinar for a course that I have built to support women to transform their lives, reliving the journey that I have once lived myself. This is something that I've dreamt of for many years, and I thought it would remain just that, a dream. But today I have brought those dreams to fruition. I cannot contain the excitement of what I have just birthed.

So why am I sitting here with tears streaming down my face? You could be mistaken for thinking that they are tears of sadness and sorrow, or a feeling of grief. However, it's quite the opposite. They are, in fact, tears of relief.

Let me take you back... back to a time in my past when I felt that I was living through hell.

Throughout my early years and early teens, I lived a life of worry, angst, and dread. I've been depriving myself of happiness throughout my life. I believe I also listened to others for far too many years of my life, including teachers, supposed friends, and partners. This was all brought on by the unhappiness and the trauma of the relationship that I had with my dad.

My dad was a troubled man and an alcoholic, living a similar life of many in his family. But the grief and trauma he suffered cascaded down to my own life and impacted heavily on the relationship that we had together.

I did not feel that I had any self-worth, and I certainly had no self-confidence or self-esteem. I went through life enduring life, rather than enjoying it and having something to look forward to. I ended school with no qualifications, believing that I was not worthy of any career in life other than the one I had been led to believe was going to be my only outcome, the only one I was capable of, which was to become an administrator for my father. A gofer, a skivvy. Little did either of us know this would never be the case.

Even though my dad passed away when I was 15, these beliefs carried on and rippled into my adulthood, I truly believed that I had no abilities or skills, always thinking that I was thick, stupid, incapable of holding any positions of worth or carrying out any skilled or intelligent workmanship. I had nothing to be proud of.

Even though I went on to achieve many promotions and accolades, I felt I did not deserve or warrant them, never had any self-confidence or self-esteem, and most certainly didn't have any self-worth. I was not capable of success, achievement, or greatness.

In 2013, I decided that I no longer wanted anybody to have my future and my worth in their hands. I didn't want anybody to dictate to me how I could and should live my life, what I was worth, what I was able to earn, or what time I could have. Then everything changed. After accepting redundancy from a job that I had been in for many years, I became self-employed, sourcing subcontracts where possible. At this point I thought that I had made it. I believed I had achieved success, but then true to life, within 18 months I lost everything, and my world crashed around my ears.

The collapse of my world

After suffering yet another blow to my world, my life as I had come to know it collapsed around me, impacting on my physical and mental health. All of my past traumas came back to haunt me, and I was at the biggest low in my life.

My core had collapsed, affecting my breathing and my ability to walk and stand, so I was shuffling around on my bottom for three months. This severely impacted my mental health, and I believed I had nothing left of any worth in my life other than my child. I had lost everything – my career, my marriage, loved ones – and it was far too much for me to endure. My mind, body, and spirit had finally given in; my body and life had collapsed and were no longer holding me up. I felt like I had nothing left to give, and nowhere to go for help or support.

After a long time of feeling worthless in life, physically and mentally devoid of any form of get up and go, I explained to a friend how I felt. I was sick and tired of being sick and tired, as this had now lasted for at least three years, The feelings of worthlessness had reached an all-time low, and it felt as though I was battling to live, battling for my life, to live and to survive.

Getting back on my feet... One step at a time

My friend suggested that I try some products she had heard of through a network marketing company, and by that stage I was willing to try anything to get my life back on track. I was starting my career and livelihood from scratch once again.

I decided to try the products, and although they were not a miracle cure, they certainly helped me on my journey of repair. I went from shuffling around on my bottom for three months to being able to walk 12 miles a day. But it all happened one step at a time.

First of all, I started with self-care, taking small walks to build up the muscles in my core as well as in my legs. I was having to visit a chiropractor twice a week and a physiotherapist once a week, and this went on for many months. But as I continued to take one step after the other, I was able to walk around a local lake. While there, I met local people who took the time out of their day to greet me, say hello, and wish me a good day, which all impacted on my mental health. It made me feel that there was something to live for, something to look forward to, and that there were kind people in this world.

From taking one step, it went to one lap around the lake, which then increased to 24 laps around the lake. Then from walking around one lake, I moved on to walk around four lakes, taking the total distance to 12 miles.

At that stage, I started to have a little hope in life, and the products that I had been taking had changed my world. As I said, this improvement impacted on my mental health and my physical health, and the more I looked after myself, the more my health improved. Walking around the lakes gave me the opportunity to think and to plan, and the fitter I grew, the healthier my diet became. Soon, the improvements in my mental health became very noticeable, and the smile was returning to my face. I had a new figure and mindset. I believed that I could change my world.

As the products had made a noticeable change in my life, I decided to become involved in the network marketing company to recommend the products, and taking part would allow me some amount of self-discovery as well as self-development. I became a distributor for the products, which meant that I was able to go out and meet other people and socialise with like-minded people. Having more positivity in my life impacted greatly on how I viewed myself and my self-worth. And with this renewed worth, I went about changing my life, which had positive effects on me for many years to come.

It was during this time I believed that I could change the trajectory of my life. Whilst watching others make changes to their life, sharing their growth and progress, I realized I was capable of doing the same myself, As a teacher, part of my job role was to deliver training, also speeches to trainees, employers and parents, so there was no reason why I could not transfer those skills and deliver speeches to those that needed to hear my story to enable them to have growth in their life.

First of all, I realised that I need to continue looking after myself. I need to fill my cup to enable me to fulfil the needs of others, and that includes creating a new career generating income/s, and building a life that I can be proud of. I can be proud of me, I can increase my self-confidence, self-esteem, and my self-worth, and never again will I have to rely on another person to do this for me. I can rely on myself, and I will have faith in me. Network marketing has been life-changing for me. It isn't for everyone, nor is being self-employed, but it has given me the ability to build a life for myself.

It was during this time as I started to believe in myself that I decided I wanted more in life, which meant I would have to return to training, to build on the skills I already had. I had to put to the test the belief and stamina which I instilled in my students, which was that if you set your mind to something and have belief in yourself, it is possible to achieve. Our mind believes what we continually tell it.

I set about laying the foundations in life, generating an income, making life easier for myself and for my family, being able to not worry about bills and scrimping and scraping, no longer living hand-to-mouth every month, Things started to become a little easier, and life was becoming more than just existence.

I am now starting to not only survive, but am coming into my own and able to thrive.

Owning my power

My personal progress has not been an overnight success; it has taken me many years to get to where I am today. I have built a life of happiness, joy, and freedom, which impacts on all areas of my life, so much so that I am now able to share that, instilling confidence, belief, love, and happiness in other people's lives. This gives me so much more confidence, happiness, and joy than I could ever explain.

I rule my world, I own my power, I am in charge of my success and happiness. No longer will I put those in the hands of others.

Finally, I have been able to banish all of my limiting beliefs.

Belief, trust and friendships

After my father passed away, I had little trust in myself or others. Life really was a struggle, for my mother, myself, and the rest of the family, and I believed that life would not get any better than that. Things changed for me, though, when I was 16 and started on a Youth Training Scheme. There I met the first person who showed any belief in me and what I could become. She entered me for competitions, and for the first time in my life I achieved qualifications. I am eternally grateful to her for all her support and encouragement, and we are still friends to this day.

From my YTS scheme, she encouraged me to apply for employment, and I was successful in my efforts. She was the one who started to instil belief in myself that I could become something and make something of my life. She was and is a godsend, and remains a guiding and shining light in my life, an inspiration to many.

After entering employment, I worked for a company that provided on-station catering. From there, I made lifelong friends, moving on in life with promotions and accolades, including awards. There are many people who supported me in life, as well as in my career, that I am still in touch with today, and we are very much a part of each other's lives – friendships spanning for more than 30 years. Without my friends and family, I would not have the strength or the belief in myself to achieve what I have to date. I have invested in myself by attending many seminars, conferences, and courses, to build and grow my skills and abilities, to widen my knowledge, and learn about self-development. Communication is key.

Chrysalis – full life circle

After delivering the webinar which left me feeling absolutely euphoric, I felt that anything was achievable. Whatever I wished to achieve was within my reach and grasp. I felt I had stepped into my power and was now ready to own my world. Whatever I believed I could achieve.

My friend who had encouraged me to plan and deliver the webinar, and who was recording me, did not realise how relevant the date was. It was not until later that evening when I told him more of my story that he reminded me of the date – 4th January, the date my father had passed away many years before. Coincidence? I like to think not.

Without two particular friends, I would not have written about this chapter in my life. Nor would I have built a course and programme. One is a friend of 30+ years who has been with me, supported, and encouraged me through thick and thin, through all of life's occasions including bereavement and marriages; the other is relatively new in my life (the last two years), but encouraged me to change my career after chronic ill health, and to utilise and transfer my lifelong skills of coaching and teaching.

And that brings me to my present. I have emerged from the chrysalis of life which I found myself in, and with love, patience, belief, and nurturing, I have metamorphosised. I have grown my wings and am now ready to fly. I have birthed a new chapter.

I have set up an exceptional programme which I absolutely love. It is my passion in life, and it has given me back my mojo, motivation, and determination to support others to rebuild their lives. I have let go. I have released pain, trauma, and abuse. I forgive myself and others.

The programme I have written, and which I am also delivering, is called Metamorphosise, which means transformation. We are all truly learning to Live, Survive, and Thrive.

Inspirational Insight

Some of the positive steps that I took to move my life move forward...

were to forgive myself for listening to others holding limiting beliefs. To counteract, this I have researched and taken part in many treatments and counselling sessions.

I wish that I had known...

what a difference and impact therapy and beliefs had on my mind and on my soul. These have huge impacts on our lives. I have forgiven myself, and my father, for our past generational traumas, and believe that my father worked hard in life and lived his life the best that he was capable of. I am grateful for all that we have been through and which we have endured throughout our lives, which is why I now let go.

I have committed myself to self-care, and I move one step forward every single day. I have changed my diet, I have changed my lifestyle, I now swim and walk every day, which is a lifestyle habit I hope to never have to give up. I have changed my mindset, and my walking round the lakes or along canals enables me to listen to podcasts. I've created vision boards, which I look at and review daily, weekly, monthly, and yearly (once again guided by the most magnificent human and teacher – so inspirational), and I have a gratitude journal. I am grateful each and every single day.

If you were/are going through similar changes or challenges in life...

I want you to know now that you are enough, you can become enough, you are able to achieve anything that you believe and wish for, anything that you set your mind to. We are what we believe we are, and we become what we believe. Should you ever need it, always know somewhere out there is a hand to hold. There is support there and people willing to support you until you are ready to support yourself.

I was Beautifully Broken.

I am now whole, I am me, version #2, still Beautifully Broken, a beautiful butterfly, resembling a broken Chinese vase carefully reconstructed with gold, shining like the sun to brighten the lives of others. I am proud of the bright, intelligent, focused, and determined woman I have become.

Soar like an Eagle, Shine like a Diamond, Rise from the ashes like a Phoenix, Emerge from your chrysalis like the Beautiful Butterfly that you are.

Dedication

To my mum, Nan, wider family, and childhood friends, without whom I would never have made it through my childhood and teens. Thank you to Pat and Ronny Ireland for always being the beacon of light in a storm. To Sharon, Lisa & Liz, thank you for always being there through thick and thin, come what may.

About the Author

Donna, who lives in Buckinghamshire, England, has been described as "inspirational and supportive".

When she is not mentoring or coaching women making efforts to improve and change their lives after reaching a crossroads in life from abuse, trauma, or illness, she can be found taking long walks in woodlands or near water – especially digging her toes in the sand and paddling in the sea, and regularly found at the local swimming pool.

She has committed the last ten years to personal growth and self-care.

Donna's mission in life is to support thousands of women to make positive, life-affirming changes to their surroundings and environment, one day at a time, enabling and supporting them to Live, Survive, and Thrive to the best of their abilities, realising goals, dreams, and ambitions they never realised they had.

Connect with Donna

admin@donnasmithcoaching.com

https://donnasmithcoaching.com

https://www.facebook.com/Donnasmithcoaching

What's Wrong With Me?

Lea Campbell

February 2020 – *My lowest point, not so Beautifully Broken (Age 49)*

"WHAT THE FUCK IS WRONG WITH YOU? GET IN THE CAR!"

What the fuck is wrong with me? I've absolutely no idea., I'm broken, a total and utter mess, I don't trust my own thoughts or judgement any more. I think I might be going mad, like stark raving mad, like I-need-to-be-sectioned mad.

I'd gone for a walk, left the house without saying anything, not thinking straight, acting erratically, then I had a panic attack, burst into tears, and phoned my partner Simon to come and get me. I was crying, then laughing – hysterical, I guess. I was scaring myself and really scaring him. I couldn't explain what it was, but something was seriously wrong with me.

This was one of the lowest points in my life. I couldn't see a way out of it, I couldn't make any sense of it, and I had no idea where to turn. I wasn't myself at all, and I thought I was mad.

I'd been made redundant from my job of 11 years a few weeks earlier, after several years of being put under huge amounts of pressure with no respect for work-life balance. I had put the way I was feeling down to work-related stress, and had been backwards and forwards to the doctor with a list of various conditions for what seemed like years. I just couldn't seem to get back on track. I lacked control in every aspect of my life, and I needed to get that control back to be able to have some order and to function properly. At least, that's what I thought.

2015-2019, maybe even earlier? It gradually crept up when I wasn't looking (Age 45-49)

I felt like I was starting to lose my confidence at work. I'd heard something on the radio about Imposter Syndrome, and I was thinking, *That could be me.* I could really relate to it, so maybe that's what was going on? Every day I had to take a deep breath, paint on a smile, and pretend I was great, but it was all an act, and I was really struggling. I'd done this job for years, so why did I feel like I couldn't do it now?

I just lived for the weekend so that I could lie in bed, do nothing, and then drink wine in the evening. I could feel my personality starting to change on a Sunday, and as the day went on I'd turn into a full-blown bitch. I'd snap at the drop of a hat, be angry and tearful, and I'd started being quite nasty. My rage would go from 0 to 100 in less than a nanosecond over the smallest of things!

I'd already been diagnosed with high blood pressure and was taking tablets to reduce that, I'd been given steroids to treat a recurring scalp issue and eczema, and I'd had the Mirena coil fitted to help with mood swings. I'd had an ultrasound after some ad-hoc bleeding to check there were no issues, which there weren't thankfully, and was given a low dose of oestrogen but not really told why. I was also on anti-depressants, yet things were still getting worse. I wasn't sleeping, I couldn't focus, my memory was shocking. I was barely functioning.

I'd also lost interest in things I used to love doing like cooking, listening to music, reading, looking after the house. It started off with small things like I stopped painting my nails or having a shave, I went to the shops with no make-up on and glasses, instead of my contacts, and my hair unwashed – all things that were, for me, unheard of! I looked in the mirror and hated myself. My eating was out of control, I was gaining weight, and I was drinking too much. I was fully aware of all of this, but I couldn't seem to stop.

At the weekends I would listen to the same sad songs over and over on repeat. I remember one evening – after much vino, obviously – I played *Chandelier* by Sia, over and over, with tears streaming down my face and sobbing uncontrollably listening to the powerful words. They totally described how I felt; it was like it was written for me.

I found it difficult to concentrate as my brain would not stop. It would just jump from one thing to another, and I was forgetting things including birthdays and family functions, and I would lose my train of through part-way through sentences. I'd put things down and not be able to find them again – car keys in the fridge, and the milk in cupboard, that kind of thing! I stopped talking to family and friends and retreated into my own little bubble. I was very sad; actually, different to sad, I can't describe the kind of despair I felt, but I had to carry on, go to work, pay the bills, and pretend I was fine.

I started to lose confidence in driving, too. Suddenly, I was terrified every time I got in the car. One morning, on the way to work, I thought things would be better if I just drove off the side of the road – I thought that a lot these days. One day, I was shaking so much I hardly even know how I got to work. Shaking seemed to be the norm, and crying; just crying all the time with exhaustion, sadness, confusion. I'd really had enough. I would sweat a lot – cold sweats, hot sweats, night sweats – and I'd noticed a change in my skin, which was spotty but with dry patches, plus I was having issues with my gums and teeth.

When the dentist said I had gum disease, I thought, *for fuck's sake, now I really am falling apart. I'm going to end up with falsies in a jar next to my bed, like my Nan did!* I'd had several urinary infections and a constant lower abdominal throb, and I kept having difficulty breathing. It was a weird sensation, like I couldn't quite catch my breath, but I thought that I was just run down and stressed out. Google was my new best friend, and I was always checking symptoms, which can be such a powerful thing in both good and bad ways.

I was being treated for so many different ailments and issues, but nothing was getting any better; in fact, most things were getting worse. It had to be work-related stress, I decided, but I could also be an alcoholic, as some of the symptoms fitted there, too, or maybe the memory loss was Alzheimer's, and was it anxiety and/or depression? The problem was that my symptoms seemed to fit with everything I looked up, so which one was it?

Then finally, I found the diagnosis. I ticked every single box, and I mean every single box, and had a lightbulb moment. Low self-esteem, fearfulness, irritability, worrying, feeling helpless, getting angry easily, withdrawing from family and friends, losing interest in favourite activities, difficulty breathing, uncontrollable crying, thoughts of suicide, trouble concentrating, insomnia, fatigue, overeating. I'd had had a nervous breakdown. The stress must have become so unbearable that my body had started to shut down.

I felt relieved, because at least now I knew what it was, and I clung onto that. But I felt so very sorry for myself, and was so ashamed that I had been unable to cope. I spoke to my doctor, and we agreed to double the dose of anti-depressants. At last, I felt I was getting somewhere. I didn't tell anyone for a while, whilst I tried to get my head around it, then I shared it with only a few very close people.

March 2020 - *Slowly but surely, baby steps*

Then there was lockdown. For me, lockdown was my saving grace, and I'm still so very grateful for it. I needed that time to repair and heal and look after me. I still needed to apply for jobs, and I could barely get out of bed before midday most days, but it did give me some sense of purpose.

I was also fully aware that exercise would help me get back into the right frame of mind, so I started to go for a walk each day. I'm lucky to live in a beautiful area with lots of stunning walks, and we had amazing weather, so the sunshine and the fresh air felt good. I had a meditation app that I hadn't used for a while, so I used that again each morning and each evening to help me start and end my day on a positive note. I had also previously gone to a yoga class that I'd loved, and due to lockdown there were now loads of online classes, so I started that up again.

One act of kindness that I remember just before lockdown, was bumping into my yoga teacher when I was signing on at the Jobcentre. Oh yes, that was a joy. The first time in my working life. I'd tried to hide from her, I've no idea why. I guess I was ashamed that I was signing on, plus I looked a total mess. However, she saw me and asked me how I was, because I hadn't been to class for a while. I burst into tears and told her that I'd been made redundant, and she gave me a huge hug and said I needed yoga now more than ever, and to come to the classes for free which made me cry even more.

Now I had a proper structure to my weekdays: start with meditation, then do yoga, apply for jobs, then go for a walk. Routine is good. I like routine, and I like lists, as this helps me to feel more in control. So I made a list of all the jobs I could do around the house, and I decided to tackle each room, one by one, with a deep spring clean.

I knew all these things would help, but I still felt like a slightly mad woman, and I still wasn't that nice to be around as my moods were pretty unpredictable. I can't even remember how or when, but one of my sisters, Jessie, asked if I listened to podcasts, which I didn't. She recommended some wellbeing ones that she really found useful, so I bought some earbuds and started to listen on my walks. OMG, why didn't I know about these before? There was so much information out there! They were really mind-blowing for me. Other people had feelings like this and issues to deal with, too! Sometimes you think it's just you, and that everyone else is living the perfect life, so it's so good to know that's a load of bollocks!

It set me on a mission to find out as much information as I could about everything mental health and wellbeing related, and that felt like another significant and positive step.

June 2020 – New Job

I applied for all the jobs I thought would suit me. I was really open to trying anything that would fit my skillset, and I had quite a few interviews over Zoom. I said out loud to nobody in particular, "I want to work for a small business locally; no more commuting, no more corporate." And shortly after, one appeared which was exactly what I was looking for. I applied, and two interviews later, got it! I started the following week. Go, girl! I was made up with myself.

October 2021 – Writing a book, what on earth are you thinking?

Fast forward a year and a bit, and although I felt tonnes better than I had, I was sure I could feel even better. At least, I was functioning almost normally again. But I could still feel a bit panicky at times and sometimes on edge and snappy, a bit paranoid, too, on occasions. I was also getting so forgetful, and the brain fog was outrageous. Often, I couldn't string a sentence together, and I'd just stop midway through because I couldn't think of the word I needed to use or what I was even talking about. I'd also made a few mistakes at work, which was not like me.

My brain went into overdrive again. Google, here we come! Were the anti-depressants making me worse? Was my dose too high, or not high enough? My blood pressure had come down and my eczema had gone, so they had been caused by work-related stress, but what about all these other symptoms I was experiencing that seemed to be getting worse?

I decided to reduce my dose, which I agreed to do gradually with my doctor. But one week in, I was panicking and shaking again, so no way was I have having that, and I just upped the dose back to what it had been. I was at my wits' end; I didn't want to be taking these for the rest of my life, but I started to feel a bit better.

About a year earlier, I'd read a book which someone in my year at school had written about a traumatic event that had happened to her whilst we were pupils. It was such an eye-opener, and I felt so sad about the lack of support she'd experienced. I was friends with her on Facebook, and she shared a post about a 5-day writers' challenge, with a view to writing a book. I read it and thought, *Why not give it a whirl?* I had plenty of things I could write about, so I did the challenge and it really fired me up – a new hobby, a new focus, something totally different. Afterwards, I decided to join the Writing Academy, which all started off positively, but then I sort of lost my way. I dipped in and out, but didn't feel my heart was fully in it.

December 2021 – Lightbulb moment!

On a rare night out that I felt up to going to, one of my other sisters, Jennie, said she was thought she was peri-menopausal – and she was three years younger than me. Had I thought that some of my symptoms could be related to that? I already had the coil fitted and was on a low dose of oestrogen, so no, I hadn't because I thought that part of things was covered. She told me about Dr Louise Newson, a menopause expert, and recommended her website and podcasts.

Well, ping went the lightbulb, the pieces of the jigsaw finally fitted together, and all the dots were joined! I could not get enough information or get through it quickly enough. I read everything on the website, downloaded the app, and listened to the podcasts – all 142 of them! It all suddenly made sense. Why hadn't it crossed my mind that maybe my HRT medication wasn't right, and anti-depressants weren't the answer? Knowledge is power – how very true.

I started to track my moods and symptoms using the Balance app, and they followed my cycle; I was always worse the week before I had a period. OMG, the list of symptoms was huge and, guess what, I had loads of them. Weirdly, many of them were the same as those for a breakdown, so had it been peri-menopausal symptoms all along, or had it been that plus a breakdown?

Symptoms that seemed unrelated were now all linked due to a hormone deficiency. Brain fog, brittle nails, breast tenderness, acne, crying, difficulty breathing, difficulty concentrating, dry skin, facial hair (Oh, what joy!), hot flushes, incontinence, irritability, itching, joint pain, low mood, low motivation, memory problems, mouth and gum issues, muscle pain, pressure in head, tired or low energy, weight gain, low libido, anxiety, abdominal pain, cold sweats, difficulty sleeping, feeling nervous, feeling tense, lack of interest in things. Who'd want to be a bloody woman!

I spoke to my doctor, who increased my dose of oestrogen and I started taking progesterone. Within

DAYS, I was starting to feel like Lea again – the person I hadn't been for a very long time.

I made sure that work knew about my menopausal symptoms and medication, so that if I was acting out of the ordinary, they would know why. I printed off information for the workplace from the website, along with symptoms, and they were really supportive.

March 2022 – Beautifully Broken

Last month, I saw that The Writing Academy was doing a collaboration book, and I really liked the idea of it. It seemed a bit less scary than writing a book on my own, so I booked a call and then totally forgot about it – literally. I missed the call and only remembered a few hours later. I booked another call and then couldn't get a signal, so I missed that one, too. I felt it wasn't meant to be, so I just thought it wasn't for me, and left it there. A few weeks later, I saw another post and that there were a few places left, but I thought, *Not this time around.*

I woke up the next morning, and the first thing that came into my head were the words 'beautifully broken'! If ever I needed a sign, that was it. So I booked a call… and here we are.

I'm still trying to get my HRT to the right levels so that I have less symptoms, and I'm on the waiting list for the Newson Menopause clinic. It's all very much trial and error, but I'm so grateful every day for coming out of the other side. I caught myself dancing and singing in the kitchen the other day, and laughed as I thought, *This is more like it. This is the Lea I know and love.*

If my story helps just one person, then writing this has been worthwhile. I want to shout from the rooftops about perimenopause and the debilitating symptoms, but also how effective HRT can be if it's the right thing for you. The positive benefits going forward are huge, as it protects against all sorts of 'old age' illnesses such as heart disease, osteoporosis, and dementia.

As I was writing this section, a song was playing on the radio which felt like another sign of confirmation. It reminded me that I am strong and invincible. I am still on my journey, but I am more determined than ever, and feel ready for the next chapter of my life.

I think that sums it up.

Inspirational Insight

Some of the positive steps I took to move forward with my life were...

Exercising regularly – Walking outdoors and yoga sessions. It had to be something I'd enjoy and stick to, tracking my steps, and making sure I achieved my move goal every day.

Focusing on my mental health – As well as exercising, reading books, and listening to podcasts, Dr Rangan Chatterjee's *Feel Better Live More* and Fearne Cotton's *Happy Place* had a huge impact on my mental health, expanding my overall knowledge and improving my outlook. I had so many "OMG, it's not just me!" moments. Meditating has helped me to focus, and journaling to get my feelings down on paper.

Food & Nutrition

Tracking what I was eating, but paying much more attention to the nutritional value of the food as well as the calories. *From The Inside Out* by Anna Anderson was a brilliant book to help with that, increasing fibre intake and reducing meat. I love to cook, so I've really expanded my go-to recipe list.

Alternative therapies

I tried a course of Reiki, and I found it amazing for feeling calm and balanced. This is something I'm going to continue with.

Last but by no means least – Medication

I'd still be in a not-so-great place if I hadn't realised that I was peri-menopausal. I did my research and went to my doctor armed with information, asked for what I suspected I needed, and took control of my recovery. The Dr Louise Newson website helped me to identify my symptoms and get the help I needed.

If you are going through any similar challenges, I want you to know...

it's all about baby steps. If you take some positive steps, ones that work for you, you will find your support network. Don't underestimate the power of talking and sharing. I've lost count of the number of times I've heard, "Me too!" You are not alone. The amount of support people are willing to provide, as well as sharing ideas and knowledge, is what has got me here today. Follow positive role models on social media; there is so much good stuff out there, so ditch the negative crap!

Trust that you will get there. There is a light at the end of the tunnel, even if you can't see it yet.

I was quite angry that this had happened to me – *And rightfully so*, I thought – but my sister Jennie said to me, "If this hadn't happened to you, then you wouldn't be in the position you are now to be able to help other people." I'd never seen it from that perspective before, so that gave me even more courage to share my story.

I was Beautifully Broken.

I am now magnificently mending! It's been so tough, but worthwhile… like every hard lesson is. I now have such a positive outlook, and I'm ready for the new chapter of my life to start at the age of 52!

Dedication

To the amazing strong women in my life who have picked me up (sometimes literally), supported, encouraged, and guided me. To my lifelong friend Chrissy, for providing me with so much tough love and advice; to my now long-distance friend Pam, who first suggested I should write a book and for providing so many laughs along the way; and to two of my sisters, Jennie and Jessie, who have been my rocks throughout the last few years. Thank you doesn't even begin to cover it; I love you all dearly.

About the Author

Lea, who lives in Ness, Cheshire, has been described as honest, enthusiastic, kind, warm, and loyal (thank you, Hannah & Noo), and someone who wants to make a difference to others because of her own experiences. When she's not in her day job, Lea can often be found trying out new ways of getting her oestrogen patches to stay stuck on, or having a little cry – generally for little or no reason (those in the know, know!). She loves to cook and experiment with new recipes, getting inspiration from the many podcasts out there covering how nutrition and gut health can benefit overall physical and mental health. She enjoys meditating, yoga, walking, and Reiki. She also loves to eat out, and appreciates a good bottle of red.

Lea has always been a bookworm and is so immensely proud to be a part of this collaboration. She is in the process of writing her first book and plans to become a published author in her own right in 2023. She is qualified in Reiki levels one and two, and is open to learning about all things that promote good physical and mental health. Lea's mission is to help continue raising awareness and removing the stigma attached to mental health and the perimenopause, especially the debilitating symptoms that some women can suffer. But more importantly, to share her story of how these symptoms can be overcome, and how life can become even better.

Connect with Lea

Facebook – **https://www.facebook.com/trying-tonavigate**

Email – campbellleaj@gmail.com

Saying Goodbye to the Ghosts

Cassandra Welford

48 hours after a Christmas I'd rather forget...

You thought you had a pretty good track record at screwing your life up, didn't you? Well, this time you have well and truly excelled yourself in expertly messing up not only your own life, but you have well and truly fucked up the future of your children. It's over, and it is all your fault.

How they will find it in them to forgive me for this, I will never know. What I do know is that I have never, ever hated myself more in my life than in this very moment. My eyes feel so raw as they sting from the uncontrollable flow of tears streaming down my face. My heart feels like it has been stabbed and ripped into so many broken pieces, and my head is throbbing with the relentless, constant beating that refuses to stop, no matter how hard I will it to go away. If only it was the physical pain I had to deal with. My emotions couldn't be any more messed up if it tried.

I can't help but wonder if the world would be better off without me around…

That dark and ugly thought doesn't stay in my head for long, but the fact it came to me has confirmed what an awful place I have found myself in. Maybe he's right. Maybe I do need to get some medical help with these dark thoughts that have been closing in on my mind, stealing the light that once shone so brightly. They have left me in a very cold and empty place that is about to get a whole lot lonelier.

I have never felt so afraid and scared in my life. At this moment in time, my only possessions are my car, my clothes, and a laptop that is on the verge of dying at any given moment. I have no money, no income from my business, and no idea what I will do if tonight is the last night in this house.

How did everything spiral out of control?

Moving in together was going to be the start of our beautiful new beginning as a family. We had firmly closed the door to our pasts as we welcomed a new future together – or so I thought. But it seems like I have ruined the blissful relationship that gave us so many happy times together. I destroyed everything with one simple sentence that came out of my mouth less than an hour ago. Why couldn't I keep my big mouth shut?

My god, how I wish I could go back time in time. If I could just take those words back, we would be enjoying another lovely evening together, blissfully unaware of the demons that had gathered in my head.

We would have had dinner as normal and be cuddled in each other's arms, watching a good movie. Instead, I am alone in the bedroom, wondering if the council will be open tomorrow so I can put my name down on the emergency housing list.

How the hell do I tell the boys we'll be leaving our house, and that their mum has made them homeless? All because she couldn't leave her past in the past and, for the first time in her life, accept that true love and happiness *can* exist.

I should have known better; this is what I do for a living, for goodness' sake. I can visualise myself now standing in front of an audience who have come to hear my uplifting true story of the journey I have been on, the lessons I have learned, and how they can do the same. I can see myself pressing the button to click onto my favourite slide that has my life philosophy written on it: "Do not allow the ghosts from your past to steal the happiness from your future."

I quickly shoot back to reality and feel like such an idiot. That same quote is written in black and white in my first book – the book that I was once so proud to have published, but would now happily burn every page of. How could I expect to hand out empowering advice to others when I can't even follow my own rules? This was further confirmation that it was time to call it a day. I definitely shouldn't be running a business; I had failed to make any profit, and nothing had gone to plan.

How could I be so stupid and naïve to think that I have what it takes to become a credible author? I must have been living in la-la land, where make believe unicorns jump over rainbows, and piss bloody glitter. I have had enough of pretending to the outside world that Little Miss Positive is effortlessly coping and getting on with life just fine – because she's not.

I have done everything within my power to try to stay strong and to move away from the darker days that I once truly believed were behind me. But oh no, they are definitely still here. Their message came out loud and clear tonight that I am still haunted by the ghosts of my past. There is no-one else to blame; it is all my fault. I have created one hell of a mess that can never be fixed. "If there is no trust, there is no relationship." The echo of these words repeat in my head over and over as I will them to stop. Lord knows I had tried so bloody hard to trust.

My heart was smashed to smithereens when I became a single parent when I was just 23 with a six-month-old baby. A few years later, I fell head over heels in love, got married, and had my second son. History repeated itself, and the devastation and destruction from my divorce was more painful than any words on this page could describe. We lost our house, and looking back I have no idea how I managed to pick up the pieces whilst promising myself that we would never be in that position of losing a house again.

It appeared the Universe didn't hear my message. Here I was, wondering if the boys' dads would let them live with them temporarily whilst I could stay with a friend and sleep on a sofa whilst we applied for a council house. My heart physically hurt at the thought of putting them through so much. When my first two relationships broke down, my parents had been a huge support, and they looked after the boys on many occasions whilst I worked or slept. I hated that they had to watch their youngest daughter fall to pieces over and over again, but I was so thankful that they could help. It was different now, though. My mum had been diagnosed with dementia, and despite loving the boys with all her heart, I had to make the heart-breaking decision not to let her look after the boys, after a serious of incidents had shown just how far she was slipping away from the women she once was.

If I was starting life again, I would be doing this on my own.

Whilst the rest of the world basked in the beautiful afterglow of their cosy Christmas celebrations, I was contemplating life as a single parent for the third time. I had never felt so alone in my life.

Merry Christmas, Cassie! This will be one that you'll never forget, that's for sure. You have screwed up something that was so beautiful, and you have broken it... forever.

Two (long) weeks later...

Waking up with agonising stomach cramps whilst heavily bleeding was not part of the plan. None of this was part of the plan. My messed-up head and life had to take a backseat whilst I made my way to the out-of-hours doctors to find out why I was unexpectedly bleeding. "You're either pregnant and having an early bleed, or you're having a miscarriage," were the words I heard as I sat alone in the surgery. After lying on the sofa for the next few days in a lot of pain, it turned out to be the latter. With my life falling apart, I have to admit that in that moment I didn't want a baby. But my god, I didn't want to lose one either…

One week later, I found out the truth.

I won't go into the full details – that would make a great episode of a soap opera – but let's just say that the relationship ending was nothing to do with my trust temporarily wavering. My intuition has always been strong. Sometimes I wish I didn't know, but I *knew.*

There is nothing that can prepare you for becoming a single mum for the third time. Once is hard, twice is devastating, three times – well, it just shouldn't happen. I didn't scream and shout, I didn't sob and wail. Instead, I sat quietly in contemplation, surprisingly feeling a huge sense of relief. To think I had been on the verge of seeking medical assistance for a mind that didn't need fixing, was scary. I may have been on the verge of losing another house, but I was not losing my mind.

There is nothing that can prepare you to sit your children down, look them in the eye, and tell them that once again their life would never be the same. I told them very honestly what had happened and that

I didn't know when, where, or how we would be moving, but I needed them to trust me. Their understanding response of, "If you're okay, we'll be okay" caused a silent tear to stream down my face.

I found myself wondering if I had the strength to carry on with my business. Could I swallow my pride and tell everyone that *The Girl Who Refused to Quit* had given up on her dreams and had actually quit? The thought left me full of dread, and actually made me feel physically sick. It shocked me that when I had lost so much and had the perfect excuse to take the easy way out, there was no doubt in my mind that I would find a way to make this work. Other people might have lost belief in me, but I had not lost belief in myself. I had to believe there was still light at the end of what felt like a very long tunnel.

Finding and moving into a new house can be stressful at the best of times, but I've learnt the hard way that not many private landlords welcome self-employed single parents with open arms. I must have put some good karma in the pot, though, as by some miracle someone gave us a chance, for which I will be eternally grateful. The huge increase in financial commitments was hard. I love the quote: 'You can find a way, or you can find an excuse.' I didn't know how, but I would find a way.

New beginnings...

If you've ever moved to a new house, you will know that this is a very stressful time under normal circumstances. But in my case, it was anything but normal.

My nerves were already hanging by a thread as I packed up our belongings, worked 12 hours a day on a new online programme, and tried to emotionally support the boys. Everything was planned, and I was counting down the days until we moved out. Then I received an unexpected call from my landlord to say that there was a problem with the boiler in the new house. It wouldn't be fixed until the following Wednesday, so he would need to postpone our moving-in date by four days.

Four days doesn't sound like a big deal, except that: a) I didn't want to stay in that house a minute longer than we had to; and b) my ex-partner was returning to the house on the Saturday, so there was no way that we were going to still be there.

The boxes were packed, the removal men were booked for the Saturday, and everything was set to be launched for my programme on the Monday. What the hell was I going to do? After a few tears of frustration, I decided that we *would* be moving out on Saturday, and my programme *would* be launched on Monday.

I needed support, and time wasn't on my side. So, I swallowed my pride and asked for help. I arranged for the boys to stay with their dads, and I reluctantly went to stay at my parents' house, after I had moved our furniture to our new house on the Saturday as planned. You may be wondering if that's a bit harsh to say 'reluctantly', but my mum's dementia had got much worse and any change in her routine caused increased anxiety and confusion. I didn't want to add to that, but didn't feel I had much choice.

After moving house alone, with two removal men who barely spoke to me, I felt exhausted and emotional driving to my parents' house. There was an emptiness in my heart.

When I arrived, Mum asked if I'd like a cup of tea. Honestly? A bottle of wine would have been my preference, but to be fair, it was only 11.30am! I told her that I would love one, thank you. Two hours passed, and I had been asked over 20 times if I would like a cup of tea, but the tea never appeared. Mum would go into the kitchen to make the tea before forgetting what she was there for and walk back out of the kitchen. Five minutes later, she would repeat the same process.

I tried to resolve the situation by offering her a cup of tea, but she would insist that she was perfectly capable of making a cup of tea... and then she'd forget again. On a 'normal' day, this was 'normal' behaviour – no cup of tea, no problem. I remember thinking how I just wanted a cup of tea and a chat with my mum. Was that too much to ask? Instead, she kept asking me over and over again how my ex-partner was. Was he at work? Was he coming over later? Where were the boys? And still no cup of tea.

In between these questions, she'd then ask me, "Do you think I'm mad? Do you think I'm demented?" I managed to deflect all of these questions, to then be faced with the question I dreaded the most: "Where's my mum? Is she dead?"

I tried with all my might to answer her questions with a calm voice and tell as many 'love lies' as I needed to, but in all honesty, I just wanted a hug and a bloody cup of tea.

One year later...

I found out about some local business funding which I was eligible for, and I was hoping it could give my business a much-needed boost. I had swallowed my pride by working two different freelance jobs, but I was not only exhausted – I still wasn't making any profit. I had been told that an adviser was going to go through a business analysis, which was the first stage of the funding application. I gave myself a quick talking to and reminded myself that this was a positive opportunity and that it would give me something to focus on. How wrong could I have been?

I was grilled by one of the most negative and condescending people I have ever spoken to. He asked me, "Why do you think your business hasn't been successful? Why aren't you making more profit? Do you really believe you have what it takes to make this work?" As the inquisition went on, my positivity and self-belief vanished.

He had no idea that I had still been hopeful of success, despite my heart breaking over Mum's condition and trying to do my best running a business as a single parent, but his infectious negativity made me question everything. Maybe he was right. Maybe I didn't have what it takes. Maybe I should just quit.

In that moment, I didn't have any more to give. I tried to explain that I did consider my business to be successful, and that I had already changed many people's lives. No, I wasn't making a huge profit, but neither were many large companies in this country! It's not easy to make a profit when you invest everything you earn back into your business. I explained that I had set up my business as a single parent, with nothing more than a £400 temporary overdraft and a social media page. I'd had to learn everything myself from scratch, which takes hard work, time, and dedication. I shared how becoming a single parent for the third time just one year ago had also impacted my business. I had found a way to carry on despite having to move to a new house and start life again.

I hung up the phone and burst into tears. I was angry with the adviser, but I was also upset with myself. His question continued to spin around in my head: "Do you really believe you've got what it takes to make this work?" As I sat sobbing in my kitchen, the honest answer was: no, I didn't. I had worked so hard to inspire people, despite my own life being turned upside down again, but I couldn't do this on my own. Where was my support? Why wouldn't anyone give me a chance?

April 2022

So much has happened since that devastating day, including my mum sadly dying from dementia in December 2020. As I write the final paragraph in my eighth book, which will be published by my company which has helped over 60 people to become authors, it turned out that I didn't need anyone else to give me a chance. I have supported myself and turned my life around through sheer determination, working my arse off, and never giving up!

Inspirational Insight

Some of the positive steps I took to move forward with my life were...

minimising the clutter in my life. Physically, I cleared so much 'stuff' that I had been holding onto, and immediately felt so much lighter. Emotionally, I have had a lot of Reiki healing, and used meditation to release trapped emotions from the past and to visualise the positive future I wanted to be part of my life.

Music has been a big part of keeping my head in the right place. Even in the lowest of the low moments, there are always certain songs that connect to my soul and uplift my mood. I now have several playlists that I listen to whilst I'm working, walking, or even cleaning the house, and have been known to have spontaneous dance parties in my kitchen!

If you are going through any similar challenges, I want you to know...

it's okay not to be okay. It's okay to ask for help, and it's okay to accept help. This does not mean that you are weak; in fact, I feel it's quite the opposite. Think about how it feels when you help someone else, and understand that those who care about you want to support you.

I wish I had known...

that some people are not meant to be part of your life forever. There are many spiritual men and women who grow and evolve through relationships. If you've had several 'failed' relationships, there is nothing wrong with you. I believe that you were sent that person to help each other. Look back at the lessons, take the blessings, and move on with your head held high. The right person is out there, and they will love you unconditionally.

I was Beautifully Broken.

I am now free from my ghosts.

Dedication

To both of my grandmas, Molly Webb and Elsie Elford. I have combined your surnames to create my company name, Welford Publishing. Through the process of a lot of healing, writing this book and breaking free from my ghosts, I have decided to embody Welford as my own surname. Your name and your energy will live on through every book that is published. Thank you x

About the Author

Cassandra, who lives in Northamptonshire, England, is the founder of Welford Publishing. She helps heart-led entrepreneurs to write and publish life-changing books.

With no degree, no writing mentor and no previous writing experience Cassandra believes there are no excuses for not sharing your message with the world.

Cassandra has published 8 books which have received over 300, 5* reviews on Amazon. She has worked as a speaker, been featured in the Daily Mail and has been invited to speak numerous times on BBC radio.

She is a proud Reiki master who can often be found relaxing by a lake or having a dance party in her kitchen when she's not creating a new generation of heart-led authors.

Connect with Cassandra

www.welfordpublishing.com

Facebook group /heartledauthors

Acknowledgements

I would like to thank all of the authors from Beautifully Broken. I am honoured that you have trusted me to become a part of your journey. You can now officially declare, 'I'm an author!' with so much pride.

I would also like to thank our wonderful editor Christine McPherson.

Cassandra's books...

The Girl Who Refused to Quit

The Girl Who Refused to Quit tells the surprisingly uplifting journey of a young woman who has overcome more than her fair share of challenges.

When she hit rock bottom for the third time Cassandra was left questioning her worth and her purpose. She could have been forgiven for giving up on everything. Instead she chose to transform adversity into triumph and with not much more than sheer determination Cassandra has now set up her own business to empower other women.

She is the girl who refused to be defined by her circumstances. She is the girl who wants to inspire other women, to show them that no matter what challenges you face you can still hold your head high, believe in yourself and follow your dreams.

She is The Girl Who Refused to Quit

Rule Your World

Reduce Your Stress, Regain Your Control & Restore Your Calm

Have you ever questioned why your head is in such a mess – even when your life appears to look so good? You know something needs to change, but don't know where to start?

When she became a single parent for the third time Cassandra feared her head may become a bigger mess than her life and inadvertently began to follow "The Rules".

Sharing her thought provoking and refreshing personal insights Cassandra's 7 rules will help to raise your self-awareness and empower a calmer, more fulfilling way of living.

Combining relatable real-life stories, and intriguing scientific studies with simple but powerful exercises, you will gain your own "Toolbox for Life" as well as admiration for this determined and strong woman.

Cassandra is living proof that when you reduce your stress, regain your control & restore your calm, you too can Rule Your World.

Share Your World

How to write a life-changing book in 60 days.

How many times do you need to be told, "You should write a book" before you finally believe that you could become an author?

Your heart wants to share your story, but your head feels overwhelmed; Where do you find the courage to start, how do you make a plan to ensure you finish, and who would really want to read about your real-life journey?

Cassandra has written a positive and practical guide for aspiring authors, who want to make a difference to the lives of others by sharing their story.

In her natural, relaxed (and brutally honest!) style of writing, Cassandra shares her simple tools and tips whilst letting you into her own inspiring, yet unlikely, story of how she became the author of three books.

Cassandra's uplifting guidance will empower you to Share Your World and write a life-changing book, in only 60 days!

I've Lost My Mum

I've Lost My Mum tells the true, soul-baring, account of a daughter who wants to make a difference to those whose lives have been devastated by dementia.

Cassandra's raw and deeply moving journey shares her own struggle for strength as well as invaluable insights into this invisible illness. This heartfelt and compelling story not only provides a deeper understanding of this cruel condition but gives hope that it's possible to find peace when someone you love is lost between worlds.

The Girls Who Refused to Quit

Volume 1, 2 & 3

In these three books, 42 women each share a chapter of their lives where they have overcome adversity.

They want you to know that no matter what challenges you face, you can hold your head high, believe in yourself and follow your dreams.

They have not only found the courage to rise from the depths of despair, they have also found the strength never to give up.

They are, *The Girls Who Refused to Quit.*

Contact Cassandra

Beautifully Broken is a collaboration brought together by Cassandra Welford who is the director of Welford Publishing Limited.

www.welfordpublishing.com

Facebook group:/heartledauthors

If you have enjoyed our book, please leave us a review as they cause joy, smiles and happy dances from all the authors!